Coventry Kersey Dighton Patmore

Religio poetae, etc

Coventry Kersey Dighton Patmore

Religio poetae, etc

ISBN/EAN: 9783337260958

Printed in Europe, USA, Canada, Australia, Japan

Cover: Foto ©Lupo / pixelio.de

More available books at **www.hansebooks.com**

RELIGIO POETÆ
ETC.

RELIGIO POETÆ

ETC.

BY

COVENTRY PATMORE

LONDON
GEORGE BELL AND SONS, YORK STREET
COVENT GARDEN
1893

PREFACE

SOME of these Essays have already appeared in the *Fortnightly Review* or elsewhere. On going over them altogether, I find that thoughts have sometimes been repeated, almost in the same words; but, as these thoughts are mostly unfamiliar and significant, my readers will be none the worse for encountering them twice or even thrice. I have drawn the materials of the Essay on Madame de Hautefort mainly from her Life by Victor Cousin.

COVENTRY PATMORE.

LYMINGTON, HANTS,
10*th May* 1893.

CONTENTS

ESSAY	PAGE
I. Religio Poetæ	1
II. The Precursor	10
III. The Language of Religion	18
IV. Attention	31
V. Christianity an Experimental Science	38
VI. "A People of a Stammering Tongue"	46
VII. The Bow set in the Cloud	51
VIII. Christianity and "Progress"	57
IX. A "Pessimist" Outlook	64
X. A Spanish Novelette	72
XI. Bad Morality is Bad Art	79
XII. Emotional Art	85
XIII. Peace in Life and Art	92
XIV. Simplicity	98
XV. Ancient and Modern Ideas of Purity	102

ESSAY	PAGE
XVI. Conscience	107
XVII. On Obscure Books	111
XVIII. "Distinction"	117
XIX. A Modern Classic, William Barnes	137
XX. The Weaker Vessel	154
XXI. Madame de Hautefort	166
XXII. Mrs. Meynell	199
XXIII. Dieu et ma Dame	213

I

RELIGIO POETÆ

No one, probably, has ever found his life permanently affected by any truth of which he has been unable to obtain a *real apprehension*, which, as I have elsewhere shown, is quite a different thing from real *comprehension*. Intellectual assent to truths of faith, founded on what the reason regards as sufficient authority for, at least, experimental assent, must, of course, precede real apprehension of them, as also must action, in a sort experimental, on faith of truths so assented to; but such faith and action have little effective life, and are likely soon to cease, or to become mere formalities, unless they produce some degree of vital *knowledge* or *perception*. I do not see what is to become of popular Religion, parodied and discredited as Christianity is by the "Religions" of Atheists, Moralists, Formalists, Philanthropists, Scientists, and Sentimentalists, unless there can be infused into it some increased longing and capacity for real apprehension.

Coleridge, at one time, proposed to write a "Religio Poetæ," with the view, I suppose, of correcting the imperceptive character of modern faith. The Poet is, *par excellence*, the *perceiver*, nothing having any interest for him, unless he can, as it were, see and touch it with the spiritual senses, with which he is pre-eminently endowed. The Saints, indeed, seem, for the most part, to have had these senses greatly developed by their holiness and their habitual suppression of the corporeal senses. But, as a rule, they do not speak, perhaps from the fear of being too implicitly believed; or, if they do, they are careful

"To make Truth look as near a lie
As can comport with her divinity,"

in order to adapt it to the public capacity. But the Poet has this advantage, that none, save the few whose ears are opened to the teaching which would be ridiculed or profaned to their own destruction by the many, will think that he is in earnest, or that his flights into regions of perception in which they can perceive nothing are other than flights of fancy. He occupies a quite peculiar position—somewhere between that of a

Saint and that of Balaam's Ass. His intellect seems capable of a sort of independent sanctification, while his moral constitution usually enables him to prophesy without a Prophet's responsibilities. The Saint dreads lest he should receive praise of men for the holiness through which he has acquired his knowledge; the Poet understands very well that no one will or ought to think the better of his righteousness for his being a seer.

The Poet, again, is not more singular for the delicacy of his spiritual insight, which enables him to see celestial beauty and substantial reality, where all is blank to most others, than for the surprising range and alertness of vision, whereby he detects, in external nature, those likenesses and echoes by which spiritual realities can alone be rendered credible and more or less apparent, or subject to "real apprehension" in persons of inferior perceptive powers. Such likenesses, when chosen by the imagination, not the fancy, of the true Poet, are *real* words—the only real words; for "that which is unseen is known by that which is seen," and natural similitudes often contain and are truly the visible *ultimates* of the unseen. "God," says Goethe, "is manifested in ultimates,"—a doctrine destined to produce some amazing developments of Christianity, which is yet in its infancy, though it seems, as it has always seemed to contemporaries, to be in its decay. The Poet, again, has, like Newton, a special *calculus*—a doctrine of infinite series, whereby he attains to unveil the infinite and express it in credible terms of the finite, showing it, if not as actually apprehensible, yet as possibly, and even certainly so, to orders of intellect which are probably only a continuation and development of our own. Of this *calculus* Dante has abundantly made use, and those passages in his Poems which we read with the most passionate delight and real apprehension are precisely those in which the argument rises from natural experience to the dizziest heights of spiritual probability. For neither in this, nor in any other Poet of like rank, is there any solution of continuity between the lowest and the highest, any more than there is in the progress of the seed from its first germination through its various transformations in seed-leaf, stem, flower, and fruit. It is still nature, but more mature nature—nature developed by successive and intelligible degrees of growth and glory, the first of these degrees being, even in this life, quite familiar to those who *know* the truth of Wordsworth's saying—

"By grace divine,
Not otherwise, O Nature, are we thine."

Again, the Poet always treats spiritual realities

as the concrete and very credible things they really are. He has no slipshod notions about the immeasurable and "infinite." He knows, as Plato knew, that God Himself is most falsely described as infinite. God is the synthesis, as Proclus declares, in his treatise on the Fables of Homer, of "Infinite" and "Boundary," and is excellently intelligible, though for ever unutterable, by those who love Him.

Another vast advantage in the Poet's mode of teaching is that it is, even in its indignant denials of negation, necessarily and always, as far as he is a Poet, affirmative and positive. "Let your communication be, Yea, Yea, and Nay, Nay, for whatsoever is more than this cometh of evil." He gives the world to eat only of the Tree of Life, reality; and will not so much as touch the Tree of Knowledge, as the writer of Genesis ironically calls the Tree of Learning that leads to denial of knowledge. He is the very reverse of a "scientist." He is all vision and no thought, whereas the other is all thought and no vision. But "Where there is no vision the People perish"; and of thought without vision it may be truly said, "Dust shalt thou eat all the days of thy life," and "dust thou art and to dust shalt thou return." The Poet could not do other than he does. All realities will sing, but nothing else will. Judge then how much reality there is, in the modern teaching of religion, by the songs of its prophets! Where in these songs is the flavour of reality, "the sweetness of the lips that increaseth learning"?

There is a kind of perception in a state of solution which must not be overlooked or depreciated. It is the substance of most of the finest lyric poetry, and of the religion of nearly all religious people, especially in these days. But this fire-mist is a very inferior form of perceptive knowledge. There is none of it in Dante. It is the "Infinite" without the "Bound," and is not sufficiently concrete to be very serviceable or communicable, being mainly unintelligent heat, though that heat may be holy. For effective teaching there must be the disc of really apprehended dogma; rays diversely reflected and refracted from clouded sources will not do. The soul *dares* not believe its own marvellous guesses and instincts, unless it can fall back upon definite dogma for confirmation and justification, nor can the corollaries of dogma, which are often of far more personal weight than dogma itself, be inferred without a definite premise.

I suppose I need not say that, by Poets I do not, in this argument, mean only or chiefly those who have written in verse. During most of the centuries which have elapsed since the beginning of Christianity the highest imaginative as well as intellectual powers of mankind have been wholly absorbed by theology and theological psychology; and I may say, without fear of contradiction from those who are at all well read in the works of St. Augustine, St. Bernard, St. Thomas Aquinas, St. Francis of Sales, St. John of the Cross, and a score of others like them, that the amount of substantial poetry, of imaginative insight into the noblest and loveliest reality to be found in their writings, is ten times greater than is to be found in all the poets of the past two thousand years put together. The vastness of the mass hinders our appreciation of its substance and altitude. Aquinas is to Dante as the Tableland of Thibet is to the Peak of Teneriffe; and the first is not less essentially a poet, in the sense of a Seer, because his language is even more austere, and without ornament, than that of the latter. It is true that the outward form of poetry is an inestimable aid to the convincing and persuasive power of poetical realities; but there is a poetic region—the most poetical of all—which is incapable of taking the form of poetry. Its realities take away the breath which would, if it could, go forth in song; and there is such a boundless wilderness of equally inspiring subject to choose from that choice becomes impossible, and the tongue of love and joy is paralysed.

To conclude, I think that it must be manifest to fitly qualified observers, that religion, which to timid onlookers appears to be on a fair way to total extinction, is actually, both by tendency from within and compulsion from without—through heresies and denials of all that cannot be "realised"—in the initial stage of a new development, of which the note will be *real apprehension*, whereby Christianity will acquire such a power of appeal to the "pure among the Gentiles," *i.e.* our natural feelings and instincts, as will cause it to appear almost like a New Dispensation, though it will truly be no more than the fulfilment of the express promises of Christ and His Apostles to the world,—promises which in every age have been fulfilled to thousands and thousands of individuals who have so learned "the King's secret" as to have become the converts of intelligible joy. Or would it be too vast a hope that such a development may truly assume the proportions and character of a New Dispensation, the Dispensation of the Holy Spirit, the Spirit of Life and perceived Reality, continuing and fulfilling the Dispensation of Christ, as His did that of the Father—the "Persona," or aspect of the Holy Trinity in the worship of the Israelites? A Dispensation under which millions instead of thousands should awake to those facts of life of which Christ said, "I have many things to say to you, but you cannot hear them yet; but when the Holy Spirit shall come, He shall teach you the things I have told you." Under the first dispensation men were the servants of God; under the second, His sons: "Sons now we are of God, but what we shall be hath not yet appeared." What if, under a third, "the voice of the Bride and the Bridegroom shall be heard again in our streets"? Our Lord, by an intervention which He declared to be premature, converted water into the wine of the Marriage Feast. He did so for hundreds, before the time of His manifestation in the flesh; He has done so for thousands who "have lived to see His coming" since. What if His fuller coming to the whole Church should be a like revelation, even in this life, for every one who so "seeks first the kingdom of God and His righteousness," that "all these things shall be added to him"?

II

THE PRECURSOR

ST. AUGUSTINE, in reply to some one who objected that there were several interpretations of a passage in Scripture besides that which the Saint had offered, replied: "The more interpretations the better." The words of Scripture and of the ancient mythologies and profoundest Poets may, indeed, be credited with containing and intending all the truths which they can be made to carry, and I do not mean to controvert any other account of the significance of the peculiar, mysterious, and, in *the letter*, unaccountable place held by St. John the Baptist in relation to the gospel of Divine Love, when I point out that the relation of Natural Love to Divine Love is represented by him with a consistent aptness and an amount of detail which can scarcely have been accidental.

In the first place he is not represented as

simply a Prophet, but as the "*Precursor*" of Christ, as Natural Love is the Precursor of the Divine. "The natural first, and afterwards the spiritual." St. Bernard says: "The love of God has its first root in the most secret of the human affections." The love between God and the soul is constantly declared to be, in its highest perfection, the love that subsists between Bridegroom and Bride ("thy Maker is thy Husband," etc., etc.), and our only means of understanding and attaining to these supernatural relations are the meditation and contemplation of their types in nature. "The unseen is known by that which is seen." "No greater than He was born of woman," *i.e.* nature; but "the least in the Kingdom of Heaven," *i.e.* Divine Love, "is greater than he"; and, as the latter increases, he must decrease. His baptism was necessary even to Christ as the representative of Christians, for none can receive effectually Christ's baptism of fire and the Holy Spirit without the previous baptism of the purifying water of natural love,—water itself always signifying, in the parabolic vocabulary of all primitive religions, the life of the external senses, or nature. Food of locusts, *wild* honey, and clothing of camel's hair are also interpreted,—by those who are most learned in that mystical vocabulary which everybody acknowledges to have been largely in use by the writers of the Scriptures as well as by those of all the great mythologies, and without which a great part of Scripture is hopelessly unintelligible,—as significant of life in natural good, of which the highest is natural love. "Honey," writes one of the most deeply learned in this vocabulary, "signifies natural good." "Locusts," says the same writer, "signify nutriment in the extreme natural," and camel's hair and a leathern girdle "denote what is natural," skin and hair being those things which are most external. St. John the Baptist is spoken of by the Church as the "strong man" and the "standard-bearer," being the mightiest of human powers, and their leader. He alone of all natural men is "sanctified from his mother's womb," and originally holy: "sole mortal thing of worth immortal." He "came to bear testimony to the light" of that Love which is the fulfilment of the prophecy of natural love. Herod, the world, was friendly to him, who nevertheless rebuked the Tetrarch for his violation of a law of natural love, and the Saint was sacrificed by him to an impure passion and the allurements of a dancing girl; which is the usual fate of pure natural love, "sanctified from the womb," when brought into conflict with the sensuality which apes and profanes it. "Let the Church," says the Service of the Saint's Day, "rejoice in the nativity of blessed John the Baptist, by whom she came to the knowledge of the Author of her regeneration." "Behold," says the same Service, "I have given thee to be the light of the *Gentiles*," *i.e.* the interpreter of the faculties and desires of the *natural* man. In virtue of his peculiar mission the Baptist compares and measures himself with Christ as no other ever did: "He must increase, I must decrease"; "He cometh, the latchet of whose shoes I am not worthy to unloose;" I am not the Christ, that *most* holy love, for whom ye, who have not yet seen Him, take me, but only the one pure mortal voice "crying in the desert" of the world, and prophesying of Him; "I ought to be baptized by Thee, and comest Thou to me?" "He was not the true light, but was to give testimony of the light." "After me there cometh a man who is preferred before me," etc.

Jesus, being baptized by John, the heavens were opened to him, and a voice from heaven said: "This is my beloved Son, in whom I am well pleased;" *i.e.* by the baptism of natural love, the heavens are *sensibly* opened to him who is already the Son of God, and Christ, as the representative of Christians, is declared then most pleasing to the Father when He has donned and assumed to Himself the *natural* life of love. Concerning the Baptist, our Lord afterwards says: "What went ye out to see? A prophet? Yea, I tell you, and *more than a prophet.* For this is he of whom it is written, Behold I send my *Angel* before thy face, who shall prepare thy way before thee," "and if you will receive it, he is Elias that is to come. *He that hath ears, let him hear.*" Our Lord says of John: "If I bear witness of myself, my witness is not true" (that is, the Divine Love cannot effectually witness directly of itself), "there is another" (natural love) "that beareth witness of me. He was a burning and a shining light, and you were willing for a time to rejoice in him." John is "the *friend* of the Bridegroom, who standeth and heareth Him, and rejoiceth with joy because of the Bridegroom's voice. This *my joy is therefore fulfilled.*" John, though naturally nearer to Jesus than any other man "born of woman" (nature) "knew him not," but by the coming of the Holy Spirit, *i.e.* divine inspiration. So natural love, though so pure an image of the divine, knows not the divine, until this is supernaturally revealed to it.

What seems to be thus obscurely shown forth as a parable in the life of the Precursor is, however, plainly affirmed by other parts of Scripture and by the doctrine of the Church concerning the significance of natural love. It is distinctly declared to be a "great Sacrament," or fact having a symbolic value of the highest consequence, as representative of the final and essentially nuptial relationship of Christ and the Church, of which every member is a church in little, with Our Lord for her head, as man is the head of woman, and God the Head of Christ. It is remarkable that, in a time when general reverence for religion is greatly diminishing, a true but altogether unenlightened reverence for the holy mystery of natural love should be sensibly increasing among us; and we may, perhaps, hail this circumstance as the precursor of a new development of Christianity which shall exert a hitherto unknown power over men, as being based upon and explanatory of their universal instincts and longings, which the symbol is, by as universal consent, wholly incapable of satisfying. And, besides the interest of the feelings, the intellect of man, which is now bent upon examining everything, must find, in the otherwise inexplicable phenomena of natural love, a satisfaction in the prospect of finding its key in another mystery which is, at least, much less inscrutable and does not involve any of the anomalies and absurdities of that passion, when it is regarded as an end having no further end. Every one who has loved and reflected on love for an instant, knows very well that what is vulgarly regarded as the end of that passion, is, as the Church steadfastly maintains, no more than its accident. The flower is not for the seed, but the seed for the flower. And yet what is that flower, if it be not the rising bud of another flower, flashed for a moment of eternal moment before our eyes, and at once withdrawn, lest we should misunderstand the prophecy, and take it for our final good? If it be other than a symbol, that is, as Coleridge defines a symbol to be, a part taken to represent the whole, then love which the heart of every lover knows to be the supreme sanity, must be condemned, by the intellect, as the supreme insanity, and its "extravagances," which, from the Church's point of view, are in the highest representative order, must be looked upon as those of a maniac who takes a green goose for a goddess and himself for a god. But all this becomes clear when the parties to love are regarded as priest and priestess to one another of the divine womanhood and the divine manhood which are inherent in original Deity. They are but ministers to each other of the "great sacrament" of that glory "which the Son had with the Father before the beginning of the world"; and the co-existence of the greatest defects, short of an absolute defect of manhood and womanhood, with a claim to the greatest reverence and devotion, has its exact analogue in the nature and claims of priesthood, as being the vehicle—and only the vehicle—of the Divine in sacramental administrations.

I should far exceed the space to which I have desired to limit myself were I to exhaust the sayings of the Scripture and the services of the Church which bear upon this interpretation of the Precursorship of John. Let me, however, point out that the great painters of the Renaissance, from Botticelli and earlier downwards—men who show, to those who have eyes to see, the most ardent interest in the hidden meanings of scriptural sayings and events,—seem to have discerned and intended to convey the substance of what I have now said, by their frequent associations of the *two* Johns, John the Baptist and John "the *Divine*," as companions and co-worshippers of the Child Jesus, their synthesis, "God made Man of the Woman," to whose maternal bosom he eternally clings.

III

THE LANGUAGE OF RELIGION

THE realities discerned by faith are susceptible of infinite corroboration, for "God is infinitely visible and infinitely credible," and, since the knowledge of God is the one end of life, the sum of human wisdom consists in the accumulation of such corroborations. Now any fresh and original testimony is thus corroborative. It is the nature of man to believe the more because another believes, and to derive additional knowledge from another's mode of knowing. But how shall such testimony be conveyed, without betraying knowledge which often cannot be attempted to be spoken without profanation by and peril to the ignorant, except in enigmas which are clear to those who know, but hopelessly dark to those who do not? Accordingly we find that the teaching of every great religion, the Jewish and Christian perhaps above all, when it once leaves the preparatory stage of natural religion and morals and formal dogma, becomes mainly enigmatical and mythical. It is quite right that popular teaching should be limited, as it is, to the preparatory stage and to the enforcement of it by Divine sanction, threats, and general promises; for the house of God must be built, the soul must know the direction in which to look for light, and must be formed gradually into sincere desire of and constant endeavour for perfection, before God can inhabit it, and baptize it with that fire without which the baptism of water lies dormant as a grain of wheat in an Egyptian tomb. It is at this point that *real religion, which is self-evident,* begins, and at this point occurs that great change in the mode of the soul's progress which is well known to Catholic psychologists. Up to this point the progression is from truth to good; afterwards from good to truth, its rule then becoming "prove all things; hold fast" (not "that which is true," but) "that which is good"; the substance becomes the guide to the form, whereas, before, the form was the guide to the substance; and at this point the Church begins to teach the soul, chiefly by enigmas, how she may best understand the instructions, and reciprocate the complacencies of that Divine Lover of whom she is henceforward the intimate companion and the living abode.

The *fact* of the existence of these enigmas lies patent to the dullest. The vision of Ezechiel (which no one was permitted to read before he was thirty years of age), Seir and Paran, in which God was, but the people knew it not; the myth given in the Breviary on the day of the "apparition of St. Michael"; the great serpent, Leviathan; the King of Egypt become King of Israel; the almost identical myth of Proteus, the sea-beast, also called "Cetes, King of Egypt"; the birth of Aphrodite; the mystery of Persephone, whose true name it was not lawful to utter, concerning which Æschylus says: "Happy is he who comprehends it, for over him Hades shall have no power"; and a thousand other such things are manifest "riddles," and were manifestly meant for such. Moreover, they are, for the most part, such *elaborate* riddles that the key which unlocks any one of them, the thought which fills up all the manifold vacuities of external sense, must be *the* key and *the* thought.

Of most such enigmas Proclus says, in his treatise on the Fables of Homer, that they are unfit for the reading of youth, to whom they are absurd, or scandalous, or worse; but that they are the proper food of age when purged by discipline from obscuring and uncontrolled passions, the co-existence of which, with the knowledge of

Divine secrets, would involve that conjunction of perceived good, with its denial by actual evil, which is more irremediably fatal to the soul than any amount of unmixed impurity. The senseless and often repulsive external word of these enigmas is as the black "veil of Moab," which God hangs before the sanctuaries of His brightest glory; and as the foul expirations of the serpent of Cos, which repelled all but him who was pure and bold enough in faith to kiss the death-breathing lips, and so convert them into those of a goddess, exhaling celestial perfumes.

Her whole system of language and rites proves either that the Church, who can speak her mind plainly enough when there is occasion for plainness, wantonly and habitually indulges in the folly of delivering a large part of her message in a language that few can understand, or that there is a body of knowledge which ought not to be and cannot be effectually communicated to all; and that, in her reticence, she is but obeying the command: "Tell not the vision to any man till Christ be risen" in him.

It would, no doubt, be of great use to many if the meaning of a few of the principal of the symbolic words common to all great religions were made a part of religious instruction; though it is wonderful how, by a sort of instinct, some of these keys are discerned and read by the simplest and least instructed of those who, among their low surroundings and labours, lead pure and meditative lives. I have heard some of our "savages," haunters of "Little Bethels," "Sions," and "Carmels," use the obscurest imagery of Scripture with an evident grasp of significance which many a Bishop might have envied. Such acquaintance with the vocabulary of symbols would not unveil anything which ought to remain veiled, while the ordinary reader and unenlightened enthusiast would be saved by it from the absurdities and scruples and often pernicious extravagances into which he now falls, through his literal adoption of words which to sensible persons are manifestly parabolic; and the student of deeper capacity would be provided with the clues without which he cannot read even the letter of the enigmas of life.

To readers of the early Christian writers the interpretation of many of these words must be familiar. The names of the four chief points of the compass, water, fire, cloud, thunder, lightning, nation, generation, father, mother, son, daughter, rich, poor, tree, stone, fish, mountains, birds, rod, flower, leaf, etc., etc., have fixed significances without the knowledge of which thousands of passages of Scripture, even those not involving any enigmatic meaning, cannot be understood. What, without such knowledge, can be made of passages, among innumerable others, like this: "The coming of the Son of Man is as the lightning which shineth from the east unto the west; for where the body is there shall the eagles be gathered together"? Or how, without such means of interpretation, can some of the direct injunctions of Our Lord, even in what is vulgarly supposed to be the plain speaking of the Sermon on the Mount, be obeyed? Of some of these injunctions, St. Augustine, rejecting the literal sense, says, in one of his sermons: "You may do these things if you can, but I cannot." From what torments might the poor simpleton of a modern pietist be saved by remembering that Our Lord "spake not without a parable"!

This mode of expressing realities by *things* having some resemblance to them, carried to the highest and fully conventionalised in the Egyptian hieroglyphic writing, was, no doubt, the origin of the similar language of Scripture, the early Church, and the mythologists, and must have been readily intelligible by the learned and those *mystæ* to whom their learning was gradually imparted. A still earlier mode of what may be called real speech may be found in those first roots of language which William Barnes and other philologists have shown to constitute a system of *phonetic* imagery —of sounds having a subtle correspondence to things. And the language of the poetry—the only *real* speech—of all nations and times, has largely consisted of a mixture of phonetic and objective imagery.

There is, besides, the more spacious imagery of parable proper, of which the external word is a consistent story, fictive or actually historic. Of this kind it may be well to point out that the Church, in her services, authorises the belief that many of the simplest incidents, even in the New Testament, have parabolic meanings of far higher value than the historic, which meanings we are sometimes called upon, in the prayers that, in the Breviary, etc., follow the recitals, to beg that "we may be made worthy to understand." Indeed, nothing can account for the emphasis and repetition with which some, extremely trivial, incidents are related in the New Testament, without attributing to the writers either the extreme of silliness and irrelevance or a wisdom of which few of us are worthy to lift the veils.

Let it be remarked that symbolic and more or less enigmatic language and rites have a high value, even when they are not intended to conceal truth from those to whom its expression would be premature. They compel, in the recipient of their teaching, a state of active co-operation, a voluntary excitement of the mind, greatly more favourable to the abiding effect of moral truths and impressions than is the state of merely passive attention. This mode of reception includes the act of reflection, without which no knowledge ever becomes our own. And here let it be said that, so far are the originators and doctors of the great religions of the world and its greatest poets from having adopted an unnatural method of teaching, that it is the very method of Nature, whose book, from beginning to end, is nothing but a series of symbols, enigmas, parables, and rites, only to be interpreted by the "discerning intellect of man," actively and laboriously employed.

The rites, customs, architecture, ornaments, and vestures of the Church are stores of more or less enigmatic teaching, and not one can be destroyed or altered without risk of some unknown loss. What have we not lost, what loss have we not to fear in the future from the vandalism of "good taste." How "natural," for example, it would be that King Humbert, if ever he thinks fit to assume possession of St. Peter's and the Vatican, should regard the erection of an Egyptian obelisk in the forecourt of a Renaissance church as a monstrous solecism in art, and so abolish one of the boldest and most impressive symbols ever devised to teach man that the " Lion of the Tribe of Judah" (with this title the obelisk is inscribed) "came out of Egypt," that the "great Serpent Pharaoh, King of Egypt" (or Nature) "is become Christ" by his assumption of the body which, without Him, is Egypt.

The Breviary, the Missal, the "Little Office," and other service books of the Church, are inexhaustible storehouses of such teaching, their leading method being the immediate apposition of passages from Scripture and the Fathers, and prayers and ejaculations which, at first sight, have no related meaning, but in which the existence of a common meaning, which is the true one, is suggested, and may be discovered by those who have the key.

Besides the forms and offices of general use in the Church, there are, and have been, local rites, which it may have been, and may still be, expedient to suppress, in favour of a wider uniformity; but of these there ought to be kept the most careful record. The dance before the altar, which still, I believe, is performed during Mass in some churches of Spain; the presentation, in other "local rites," to the officiating priest of the bread by a maiden and of the wine by a youth; and the like "customs" are all acted words of more or less significance, and are sometimes more interpretative of the Church's doctrine than any written speech.

Of course, the enlightened students of the magazines will laugh at the notion that there is any knowledge which can or ought, for their own sakes, to be concealed from them. I must content myself with the perhaps irrelevant remark that those who have hitherto been reputed the wisest have, in all ages, used and recommended such reticence, and would have understood and commended Aristotle when, in reply to Alexander's complaint that, in a certain book, the philosopher had published "secrets," he said: "They are published and not published, for none will learn from my book anything but that which he already knows." And I will add that, neither in ancient nor in modern times has there been a poet, worthy of that sacred name, who would not have been horrified had he fancied that the full meaning of some of his sayings could be discerned by more than ten in ten thousand of his readers.

The denial by Mr. Grote and his followers that there is any parabolic or enigmatic meaning in the ancient mythologies is a most astounding proof of how men, of common sense in most things, will persistently deny, in the face of what ought to be absolutely convincing evidence to the contrary, that there may be anything to be understood in that which they cannot understand. It must be conceded, of course, that the teaching, if teaching be intended, in the Greek myths, is most unsystematic, and that the successive additions and modifications of the Homeric mythology, introduced by the Hesiodic and Orphic schools, brought in much confusion of names and attributes; but what is this against the presumption of a generally intelligent character in a mass of stories which, if it does not consist mainly of riddles, is as amazing, in its alternative character of incongruous nonsense, as the most enthusiastic neo-Platonist would have it to be, in the character of a storehouse of psychological observation, a *Summa Theologiæ* of the great religion of which *Scire teipsum* was the first injunction, as it is, indeed, of Christianity. That Lord Bacon, and many others before and after him, should have given, as Taylor the Platonist says, "frigid and trifling interpretations" of the Greek myths, is surely no excuse to Mr. Grote and others for maintaining that a riddle, which is on the very face of it a riddle, has no answer.

On the other hand, what rational mind can see anything irrational in the belief that, to a race ardently believing in the Divine and in the capacity of man for Divine communications, every god and goddess represented a particular aspect of divinity towards the soul; and the soul, in each of its moods, activities, and capacities, some goddess or mistress of the gods; and that the adventures of gods, goddesses, nymphs, and heroes should often be parables of the phenomena of interior experience, experience too pure and subtle for common acquisition, and too sacred to be exposed to vulgar curiosity? And who are the best authorities upon the question, whether such significance was intended or not? Shall we follow Mr. Grote and the modern "scientists," with their "congenital incapacity" for spiritual realities, or Æschylus and a hundred others before him, who averred that these stories were life-giving mysteries, and the law-givers of their time who decreed the punishment of death against those who should explain them to the multitude?

The charge so often brought against the Church of having drawn upon these sources of illustration ought to constitute one of her highest claims to the admiration of a "liberal" age; for it amounts to this, that she alone has dared to recognise truth as canonical, wheresoever it may be discovered, and that she has not hesitated to appropriate the gold and silver vessels of her enemies, when they, of all others, were found fittest to contain the corresponding goods of spiritual perception and truths deducible from her faith. Nay, was not the Vine itself " brought out of Egypt," which, " when it had taken root, filled the land" of her former captives, and vivified with the inebriation of natural and intelligible hope, the faith that would otherwise have been too spiritual for man? The Church does not dwell so often and emphatically on the coming of Christ "out of Egypt" for no reason. The designers of the first Cathedral of Christendom were not guilty of a ridiculous solecism when they placed an Egyptian obelisk at its entrance, or of utter vacuity of meaning when they inscribed it with the title, "The Lion of the Tribe of Judah."

IV

ATTENTION

ATTENTION to realities, rather than the fear of God, is "the beginning of wisdom"; but it seems to be the last effort of which the minds, even of cultivated people, are at present capable. No good and excellent thing requiring the least act of sustained attention to reality has any chance of recognition among us; original insight is dead, and men can see only the things which others, in less hasty times, have seen before them, and even these they can scarcely be said to see with their own eyes. Were the *Divine Comedy* to appear for the first time now, it would never be heard of, except in the small-type notices of the literary papers in which the young man who criticises poetry—because he has not learned to do anything else—would hasten to avail himself of so rare an opportunity of being funny. The faculty of attention to a line of scientific reasoning is common enough. It is the capacity for looking steadily at realities worthy of being reasoned about which is wanting. Through this impotence of attention, psychology has come to be a science the first axiom of which is that there is no soul, a denial which seems commonly to be owing, not so much to the vicious interest of corrupt passions, as to physical impatience of the attitude of attention demanded for the contemplation of human realities. Even the meats and wines of the epicure's table cannot be enjoyed without the habit of attention; hence the epicure's table is no more. Wealthy givers of dinners now trust, with scarcely any danger of discredit, to their guests' swallowing with applause whatever dainties are set before them, provided the consequent headache or colic is not immediately referable to its cause.

Much less will the nectar and ambrosia of the natural affections, for example, yield their flavours to the palate, "studious to eat and not to taste." Through want of attention, more often, perhaps, than through inveterate vice, how many tread into the mud, with the foolish hoof of their lusts, the very flowers after which they are for ever in frantic search; and almost all men now bewail the impossibility of attaining the poor dolls which they dignify by the name of their "ideals," when Nature, "if we do but open and expand the eye," is always actually excelling every imagination of beauty; and realities, far lovelier than any "ideal," stand about us, willing to be wooed and longing to be won.

At least once in a lifetime, and by some hitherto unexplained awakening of full attention for a little while, what man but has seen a woman, and what woman a man, before whom all their previous "ideals" have paled; and if, by subsequent nearness, they get within the eyes' focus and the vision is dimmed, that is the fault of the eyes, and no discredit to the reality of the thing seen, as is proved by the way in which death restores the focus, and with it the vision. Attention, however, as multitudes have confessed with fruitless tears, would have adapted the focus of the eye to the nearness of the object, and made it more, not less, lovely by closer inspection.

Through inattention to their own true desires and capacities, men walk, as in a dream, among the trees of the Hesperides, hung with fruit the least taste of which includes the summed sweetness of all the flesh-pots of Egypt, yet so far surpasses it as, once tasted, to supersede for ever the lust of the eyes, the lust of the flesh, and the pride of life; but they do not dream of plucking them. The letter of Scripture is like the walls of a furnace, unsightly, and made of clay, but, to those who attend, full of chinks and crevices through which glows the white heat of a life whose mysteries of felicity it is "unlawful to utter"; but religious people are in too great a hurry of spirit to see anything but the clay walls, and they lead mean and miserable existences while loudly professing the faith which "hath the promise of this life also."

The hour or half-hour of daily "meditation," or attention to his own business, which used to be the practice of every good man, is now unheard of unless it be in Monasteries. The best among us, wholly unconscious that men can advance the world's improvement only by attending to their own, are busy about everything but that which concerns themselves, and after their dusty and profitless day's work they go, as Coleridge says, to the Divine Master for *a*-musement. Hence, among many other unprecedented phenomena of our day, there is an almost complete lack of men of letters. We have only newspaper, magazine, and booksellers' hacks; clever enough, indeed, but without insight, character, or any care for a desire to propagate a knowledge of the true realities and delights of life.

Yet how vast are the rewards of a habit of attention, and how joyful an answer can the few who still practise it give to Wordsworth's question:—

> "Paradise and groves
> Elysian, Fortunate Fields—like those of old
> Sought in the Atlantic main—why should they be
> A history only of departed things,
> Or a mere fiction of what never was?
> For the discerning intellect of man,
> When wedded to this goodly universe
> In love and holy passion, shall find these
> A simple produce of the common day."

The habit, however, of such attention to realities as I am speaking of, is not to be formed without pain in those who have it not, unless they are possessed of mind and conscience, and something of the spirit of the child, that—

> "Mighty Prophet, Seer blest,
> On whom those truths do rest,
> Which we are toiling all our lives to find."

The soul which wants these qualifications, and has long dwelt easily and pleasantly and, perhaps, without external offence, in unrealities, finds itself, when it endeavours to face reality, filled with an anguish of impatience, and rushes to and fro in the prison of its customs, like a caged wild beast. There are thousands, however, who are not altogether so disqualified; and these, if they only looked, would "see in part and know in part" those eternal entities which, if not so seen and known now, will never be seen and known.

"Blessed," cries the Substantial Wisdom, "is he who explains me"; adding, in words of piercing but disregarded sweetness of invitation: "*Deliciæ meæ esse cum filiis hominum.*" With her, as with a mortal mistress, the one unpardonable crime is want of "attention."

It is not to be supposed, however, that the celestial secrets with which she rewards her steadfast votaries are to be attained, even by such as are naturally not disqualified, without considerable sacrifice of meaner goods. In the eyes of fools there is no such foolishness as the knowledge of things of which they know and can know nothing; and from such he who attends faithfully to his own true business will probably have much to suffer; for they will not be content with despising him for his infatuations, but they will hate him and do him what harm they can. He will also have to sequester himself from many natural and innocent interests and pleasures, in order to have time for the great learning, which is usually of slow acquisition, and the result of patient listening and of the hardly acquired habit of suspending *active thought*, which is the greatest of all enemies to *attention;* for "good thoughts are the free children of God, and do not come by thinking." He will also have to suffer from ordinarily good and well-intentioned people the charge of narrowness of benevolence, as well as of intellect; for he will have no time or energy to spare for seeking out and serving other objects of charity, seeing that the knowledge of his own supreme needs will be increased by every day's addition to his immense but incommunicable treasure; incommunicable, indeed, now, but, as he learns from the Church, an addition to the everlasting treasure of all who are united with him in the "Body of Christ." Not that he will really be inoperative in the time being for good to others; for the mere life, however retired, of one in habitual communion with Wisdom, breathes a sphere of wisdom which extends far beyond its definable bounds; and, as for the "narrowness" with which he is charged, he may answer that the power of cleaving is in proportion to the narrowness of the edge and the weight at its back; and that the least of his words or actions may be of more effect in the world than the life's labour of any of the herd of good people who are "busied about much serving," instead of sitting attentive at the feet of Truth.

V
CHRISTIANITY AN EXPERIMENTAL SCIENCE

CHRISTIANITY is an experimental science, and the best answer to one who questions, If it be true, is, Try it. But one difference between this and other experimental sciences is, that the necessary course of experiment is almost always, in the beginning at least, extremely difficult, painful, and repugnant to nature. Another is, that the result, though, provided this course be conducted with full sincerity and patience, sure to be absolutely convincing to the experimentalist, will not be wholly communicable or convincing to anybody else. It will give, indeed, to the person who has attained it, certain characteristics of manner, speech, and action which will strongly tend to impress any honest man that the experiment may be worth trying on his own behalf; but that is all.

The experiments and conclusions of the natural

sciences can be discerned and judged by the natural senses, which all men have in common, and which have no interest in being blind to the facts of nature. But the spiritual senses, except in the exceedingly rare cases of some men of genius, in whom they appear to exist independently of the moral perfection which is their commonly indispensable condition, have scarcely any life in the great mass of men, who live, often virtuously, or at least decorously, contented with knowing and enjoying only in their natural shadows those realities which are devoutly and substantially discerned by that higher order of perception which is usually the ultimate reward of so "doing God's commandments" that we may "know of the doctrine."

The multitude, Catholic and otherwise, who are, as Sir Thomas Browne says, "incapable of perfectness," have branded this science with the name of "mysticism." Cardinal Wiseman, accepting the name, defines "mysticism" as being "the science of love." What wonder if experimental knowledge in this science should be scarcely at all accessible to the vast majority of souls, in whom the seed of love has never yet passed beyond its rudimentary and apparently opposite state of fear, and who really regard the very notion of personal love to God and delight in

communion with Him as a sort of irreverence,—
which, in them, indeed, it would be! There is,
in fact, no Church but one which, as a rule,
ventures even to propose this kind of love as the
end and crown of its teaching. St. Evremond
says that the most characteristic difference between that Church and all others is that, while
the one makes it the ambition of the soul to
please Him, the others seek only to avoid dis-
pleasing Him; love being the principle in the
one case, fear in the other. The "science of
love" is, indeed, "mysticism" to the many who
fancy its experiences—incommunicable as the
odour of a violet to those who have never smelt
one—to be those of idiosyncratical enthusiasm or
infatuation; but, among "mystics" themselves,
the terms of this science are common property.
Deep calleth unto deep a prophecy which is not
of "private interpretation," but one which has a
language as clear as is that of the sciences of the
dust, and as strict a consensus of orthodoxy. A
St. Catherine of Genoa and a St. John of the
Cross know each what the other is saying, though,
to a Huxley or a Morley, it is but a hooting of
owls.

There are infinite degrees of this experimental
knowledge, from that first sensible "touch" of
God's love, which usually accompanies the first

AN EXPERIMENTAL SCIENCE 41

sincere intention of perfection for His sake, to that of the Saints who have united themselves to God by a series of agonising initiations of self-sacrifice, and by years of actual and habitual perfection of obedience in the smallest as well as the greatest things; and, further still, to the knowledge of the angels, whose purification and consequent capacity goes on increasing for ever. But the very first sincere experiment, and its perceptible result, though they may be followed by years and years of relapse and seeming failure, are generally final. The man who has made the experiment has seen God; and that is an event which he will never be able altogether to forget or deny, a positive fact which, for reality and self-evidence, stands alone in his experience, and which no amount of negative evidence will be able, even for a moment, to obscure.

For this first experiment of faith, a belief in a personal God and in His right to command and judge us is the only dogmatic ground which is required, and this ground almost every form of religion affords; and that "touch" of love which, as the Church says, "supersedes all the sacraments," is given to each one, who, with all his heart, even for an hour, submits himself to the guidance of the "Light which lighteth every man who cometh into the world." If his memory clings, with however poor a fidelity, to that first kiss of God, that baptism of fire which is the tacit knowledge of the Incarnation—for is it not God made one with His body, *i.e.* his senses—that initiating perception that God *is* will lead him into further actual illumination, in proportion to his fidelity and to the amount of Catholic dogma which his particular Church may be capable of teaching—for fidelity does not *discover* dogma, but only enables the faithful, in proportion to their faith, to confirm it with absolute personal assurance. *False* dogmas cannot be believed with this experimental certainty, because they do not represent realities; therefore such dogmas will not be believed by any one who has seen God, in such a way as finally to hinder the saving power of the true teaching. Thus, in Churches and sects which teach dogmas in themselves subversive of all morality and right belief in God's nature and government, we find individuals so deeply rooted in the fundamental orthodoxy of love, that, while daily professing with their mouths the immoral and pernicious doctrines of their sect, they so deny these *doctrines* in their hearts and lives, that the only harm—a very great one indeed—which befalls them from this position, is the impossibility of adequately developing their own nature. Each great Catholic dogma is the key, and the only key, to some great mystery, or series of mysteries, in humanity; and, this dogma wanting, the humanity of the individual is so far deprived of the means of eternal development; which must be initiated in this life, if at all. But, in any case, provided he has attained "to lay his just hand on that golden key which opes the palace of eternity," by absolute fidelity to his best light, the *truths*, which he has adopted by faith, become "*res visa et cognita*," in a sense of which Lord Bacon did not dream; for Lord Bacon's "philosophy," as philosophy, was even baser than his political career, and it did not deal with "things," which are the objects of Wisdom, but with phenomena, which are only hints and corroborations of realities discovered by that which is philosophy indeed.

A duck-pond, however, must not be expected to grow salmon or pike, and the offspring of the conventicle will always remain narrow, in his possibilities of experimental knowledge, as compared with those who have been fed in the larger waters which occasionally bring forth a Hooker or a Keble, as these are when compared with the ocean-brood of Austins, Bernards, and Theresas.

But, wherever the elementary dogmas of Christianity are taught, there the man who is *perfectly* sincere and faithful is in the possibility of an infinitely precious experimental knowledge; and that knowledge, however limited (and the knowledge even of the angels is limited), will fit him for his destined place in the communion of Saints; and may raise him far higher in God's favour than other Saints who may have discerned and loved a wider truth, truly, indeed, but with less intensity. Such men are Christ's beloved "poor" (not the world's "poor," who are quite as proud, vicious, luxurious, and covetous of this world's goods as the world's "rich"), and, though they have been fed only with crumbs from the table of those who sit at feasts of the fullest orthodoxy, such crumbs will nourish in them a life which the merely "wise and learned" in the letter of divine truth can never know.

To such a man the Incarnation becomes, not the central dogma of his faith, but the central fact of his experience; for it is going on perceptibly in himself; the Trinity becomes the only and self-evident explanation of mysteries which are daily wrought in his own complex nature, the result of the *fiat*: "Let us make man in our own image," and he finds in his soul and body the answer to the prayer, "Let me so behold Thy presence in righteousness, that I may wake up after Thy likeness and be satisfied with it." Like Teiresias, he has seen the unveiled wisdom, and thenceforth can see nothing else; his guide is thenceforward, not formal laws or truths which can be uttered, but the golden rod of a supreme good, which leads him infallibly (and most sensibly) by glowing into greater felicity so long as he is in the right path, and by fading, more or less, as he is in danger of error. Like Teiresias, again, on the mountain heights of contemplation, persevered in through years and years, he strikes, from time to time, with his golden staff upon interwoven mysteries of nature, and finds in them the revelation of undreamt-of secrets of his own being; and he finally becomes, not so much an adorer as an actual participator in the nature and felicity of that Divinity which alone " has fruition in Himself," and "who became man that men might become gods."

VI

"A PEOPLE OF A STAMMERING TONGUE"

In things of the spirit we can only "see in part and know in part" and "as in a glass darkly." Hence, in writing concerning these things, the aphoristic manner always has been and always will be found the most proper and fructifying. In spiritual philosophy the blessing of systematic perfection has ever been paid for by the curse of barrenness; for between the facts of the science of the soul there is often no visible continuity and sometimes an appearance of contradiction; and in such cases we have to be contented with the simple perception and affirmation that they *are*. Again, such facts, in proportion to their importance, are simple and self-evident; and, in proportion to their simplicity and self-evidence, they are, as Aristotle says, apart from the domain of the reasoning faculty, and therefore unintelligible and incredible to those who have acquired the habit of relying, not upon reason, but upon reasoning, for proof. Nothing can be more express than the way in which this is over and over again asserted and implied by Our Lord and His Apostles. "None can say that Jesus is the Lord but by the Holy Ghost," that is, by the spirit of direct vision. "I tell you these things, not because ye know them not, but because ye know them." "The Holy Ghost shall *teach* you whatsoever I shall have *said* unto you," etc.

Dogmatic truth is the key and the soul of man is the lock; the proof of the key is in its opening of the lock; and, if it does that, all other evidence of its authenticity is superfluous, and all attempts to disprove it are absurd in the eyes of a sensible person. That only a very small proportion of the human race should be capable of at once receiving self-evident truth is quite natural. The key is not less the key because it will not open a lock of which the wards are filled with stones, and rusted by disuse or destroyed by sin. "Authority" comes in here. When a man "speaking with authority," that is, with the indescribable air and character which is an unmistakable claim to being listened to, affirms things beyond all ordinary experience and credibility, and adds that it is only by "doing the commandments" that we can "know of the doctrine," a sincere and businesslike mind will at least consider the experiment of that moral perfection to which such wonderful things are promised worth trying; and, if he tries with full integrity of purpose and persistence, all persons who have reached that perfection assure us that he will not fail to attain to that direct vision to which truths, received on "authority" as "dogmas," gradually become discernible as *facts*, "infinitely visible and credible" (as St. Augustine says of God) and of incomparable personal interest to himself. The infinite visibility and credibility of such facts implies a counterpart of infinite invisibility and incredibility. "The angels themselves desire to look into these things" and to fathom them fully, but in vain. The higher they soar in the light of vision the more manifestly incomplete and "unsystematic" is their theology; and their knowledge becomes more and more merely and absolutely "nuptial knowledge," that is, the knowledge of fruition, for which there is no intelligible word nor "reason."

When the soul has passed the "purgative" stage of obedience to law, and has attained the "unitive" condition, in which all fidelity is habitual and comparatively easy, she becomes capable, for the first time, of real "insight," and knowledge ceases to be acceptance of "dogma" so much as personal communion. She exclaims, "The Lord hath fashioned me and laid his hand upon me"; but she adds, "Such knowledge is too excellent for me; I cannot attain unto it"; and the utterances whereby she endeavours to draw others to her wisdom are interjections, doxologies, parables, and aphorisms, which have no connecting unity but that of a common heat and light.

Another reason for the inadequacy of expression in the science of the soul is the "unlawfulness" of speech concerning some of its most essential facts. St. Paul, in his vision, says he saw things which it was, not impossible, but "unlawful" to utter. Again, the spectators of the Transfiguration were commanded not to tell the Vision to any man until Christ should be risen, that is, until Christ should be risen in their auditor, it being lawful to speak of the mysteries revealed in that Vision only to those who already know. Again, the Bridegroom of the soul loves to reserve to Himself the office of her instructor in His secrets; and the more she has learned the less will she be willing to speak. "My secret to me," is the reply of the Saints to inquirers concerning their peculiar knowledge. "Night," says the Soul, "is the light of my pleasures," and she refuses by speech to obscure them with the darkness of day. Furthermore, her confession of such knowledge involves incurring the praise of man for having corresponded with peculiar fidelity to the graces of God; and she abhors the praises of any but Him, whose assurance that He "greatly desires her beauty" makes all lesser laudation profane and disgusting.

Besides the pride and modesty of the pure soul, there is yet another reason why those who know most speak least. There comes a time to those who follow perfection, in which all possible forms of beauty are, as it were, discerned at once; it is not beautiful things, but Beauty itself which is perceived; and in the light of this faint aurora of the great and unspeakable vision, all particular forms of beauty, such as quicken the tongue of Art, fail to arrest interest and attention and the desire of communicating them to others. A sculptor who could see, at one moment, all the possible forms of beauty which might be wrought from his block of marble would be quite unanxious and unable to develop any one of them.

VII

THE BOW SET IN THE CLOUD

It may be a matter of surprise to many that I, professing to be an orthodox Christian, should frequently use language which seems to assume that some knowledge of Christian mysteries has been enjoyed by individuals in all times and places, that the light which lighteth every man who cometh into the world shone, more or less obscurely, before the days of Him who came to bring light into the world; but this is a belief and a conviction which is growing more and more general with the growing light which the contemplations of Saints and Doctors has cast upon Catholic doctrine; and it need present no great difficulty to the mind, however scrupulous to keep within safe limits of faith, if it be borne in remembrance that the Incarnation was an act done in eternity as well as time; that the Lamb, the "I am before Abraham was," was "slain from the beginning"; and that, if we look from the point of view of eternity, we may see that effects of that act apparently retrospective were not really so; but that the Bread and Wine, without which "there is no life in us," may have been received from the hand of an invisible Melchisedech by many who, in time, have longed to see the Day of the Lord, and have done their best, by heroic purity and self-humiliation, to merit the Vision, and have thus attained to that love which, as St. Augustine says, "supersedes all the sacraments."

Nor do glimpses of the heavenly vision seem to have been absolutely denied to any race of men. The general "darkness that comprehendeth it not" seems occasionally to have been lifted among races whose night is by most good people presumed to be total. The religious rites of some "savage" nations sometimes startle those who know the meaning of the rites of the Church by a strange identity of significance. God's mercy is over all his works, and he does not refuse to such babes and sucklings some effectual hints of that knowledge which is especially promised to babes and sucklings, and denied to the wise and learned. Finally, let me note that the anthropomorphic character which so universally marks the religion of the simple, and is so great a scandal to the "wise," may be regarded as a remote confession of the Incarnation, a saving instinct of the fact that a God who is not a man is, for man, no God.

The mystery of triple Personality in one Being, the acknowledgment of which is the prime condition of a real apprehension of God, may be best approached by the human mind under the analogue of difference of sex in one entity; as it was by Plato and by much earlier Greek Philosophers, and, more or less obscurely, by the " wise ancients" of India and Egypt; and, for the first time, quite clearly shadowed forth by the Scriptures and the Church; Nature herself adding her crowning witness, without which men are incapable of effectually grasping any spiritual truths. "In the beginning" (*i.e.* before men had lost their original knowledge of God and His Image in Man) "there were," says Plato, "three sexes." The saying, "God is a beautiful Youth and a Divine nymph" is attributed to Orpheus. By the Church the Second Person is represented as the "glory" of the "Father," who is Christ's "Head," as Man is the glory of his Head, Christ, and Woman the glory of Man, who is her head. The individual Man, the *homo*, is the Image of God in so far as he is a substantial reflection of the Love, the Truth, and the Life, which last is the "embrace" of Truth and Love, as the Holy Spirit is said by the Church to be the "embrace" of the First Person and the Second. And nature goes on giving echoes of the same living triplicity in animal, plant, and mineral, every stone and material atom owing its being to the synthesis or "embrace" of the two opposed forces of expansion and contraction. Nothing whatever exists in a single entity but in virtue of its being thesis, antithesis, and synthesis, and in humanity and natural life this takes the form of sex, the masculine, the feminine, and the neuter, or third, forgotten sex spoken of by Plato, which is not the absence of the life of sex, but its fulfilment and power, as the electric fire is the fulfilment and power of positive and negative in their "embrace."

Man (*homo*), according to the writer of Genesis, originally contained the woman, and was in his individual self the synthesis; and the separation into distinct bodies has been regarded by some theologians as a consequence of the fall, from which the regenerated will recover, in that state in which there is no giving or receiving in marriage, man (*homo*) himself *being* a marriage and "as the angels in heaven,"—a change which is already foreshadowed in the "Brides of Christ" by that which is their most sensible characteristic, namely, a marked increase of the feminine nature, which is passive, humble, receptive, sensitive, and responsive; this increase, however, so far from being at the expense of the masculine character, that this latter is exalted into fuller strength, invincible courage, and greater wisdom to command all that is below him, especially his own feminine nature—whose rebellions, in his natural condition, are the cause of all his disasters.

"Receive thy glory" (womanhood "the glory of the man") "with joy," says St. Paul to those who had newly seen the unveiled wisdom; and, in the wonderful parable of Teiresias, that change or rather discovery in his own nature was the first effect of the same vision, which blinded him, as it does any one who has beheld it, to all other objects of sight. This three-coloured Iris (the "Messenger of Juno," the Divine womanhood), is also the "Bow set in the cloud" of the renewed nature, for a promise that it shall never again be overwhelmed and destroyed by the deluge of the disordered senses.

According to Christian theology, it was the Second Person, the "glory" of God the Father, who took on actual womanhood or "body" in the body of the Blessed Virgin, and who imparts the same to all who partake of the same body in the Holy Sacrament; and accordingly it is said by St. Augustine, that "Christ is the Bride as well as the Bridegroom, for He is the Body"; and St. John of the Cross says that, in the last heights of contemplation, man attains to contemplate Him as the Bride, an attainment corresponding to the second change of Teiresias after his seven years of meditation on the first.

VIII

CHRISTIANITY AND "PROGRESS"

MANY people doubt whether Christianity has done much, or even anything, for the "progress" of the human race as a race; and there is more to be said in defence of such doubt than most good people suppose. Indeed, the expression of this doubt is very widely regarded as shocking and irreligious, and as condemnatory of Christianity altogether. It is considered to be equivalent to an assertion that Christianity has hitherto proved a "failure." But some who do not consider that Christianity has proved a failure, do, nevertheless, hold that it is open to question whether the race, as a race, has been much affected by it, and whether the external and visible evil and good which have come of it do not pretty nearly balance one another.

As to the question of the real failure or success of Christianity, that must be settled by considering the purpose of its Founder. Did He come into the world, live and die for "the greatest happiness of the greatest number," as that is commonly understood, and as it constitutes the end of civil government? Was it His main purpose, or any part of His purpose, that everybody should have plenty to eat and drink, comfortable houses, and not too much to do? If so, Communism must be allowed to have more to say for itself, on religious grounds, than most good Christians would like to admit. Did He expect or prophesy any great and general amelioration of the world, material or even moral, from His coming? If not, then it cannot be said that Christianity has failed because these and other like things have not come of it. In these days all truth is shocking; and it is to be feared that the majority of good people may feel shocked by the denial, even in His own words, that such ends had anything more than an accidental part in His purpose or expectation. He and His Apostles did not prophesy that the world would get better and happier for His life, death, and teaching; but rather that it would become intolerably worse. He foretells that the world will continue to persecute such as dare to be greatly good, and that it will consider that it does God service in killing them. He tells us that the poor will be always with us, and does not hint disapproval of the institution even of slavery, though He counsels the slave to be content with his status. His mission is most clearly declared to be wholly individual and wholly unconcerned with the temporal good of the individual, except in so far as "faith hath the promise of this life also"; and moreover, and yet more "shocking" to modern sensibilities, He very clearly declared that, though He lived and died to give all a chance, the number of individuals to be actually benefited by His having done so would be few; so that it was practically for these few only that He lived and died. That may be very shocking; but they are *His* words, and not mine, and those who do not like them should have a special edition of the New Testament revised for their own use, from which all disagreeable references to the many called and few chosen, the narrow way which few find, the broad road generally taken, and the end it leads to, etc., etc., should be excised. It is not to be denied that our Lord's doctrine must be in the highest degree unpleasant to all who will consider what it really is, and who have not the courage either to reject it or adopt it in a whole-hearted manner.

But has Christianity failed in doing that which alone it professed to do? It has not, and has not professed to improve bad or even indifferently good people, who form the mass of mankind, but it does profess to do great things when it is received in "a good and honest heart," that is, in the heart—according to Hamlet's estimate—of about one in ten thousand. The question, then, of failure or success narrows itself to this : Has Christianity done great things, infinitely great things ; and has it all along been doing, and is now doing, such things, for the very small proportion of mankind with which it professes to be effectually concerned ? Professor Huxley says frankly, No. It emasculates and vitiates human character ; and he exemplifies his position by the example of the Saints of the order of St. Francis. It is well to have such a good, bold statement of opinion. Here is no shilly-shallying, and we now know that there are some persons, of strong common sense, who think that Christianity *is* a failure, as having failed to carry out its professions. Few persons who are in their right wits would choose to seek a fencing-match with Professor Huxley. They might be altogether in the right, and yet, as Sir Thomas Browne says, they might come off second best in the conflict. In any case, it is not at present my affair. It is enough for me to point out that it is conceivable that there are sciences, even "experimental" sciences, in which Professor Huxley has not yet qualified himself to be considered as an expert. Christianity professes to be such a science, a strictly experimental science, only differing, in this character, from chemistry, inasmuch as the experiments and their conditions can, in the one case, be easily fulfilled and judged by the senses which are common to all men; whereas, in the other, they are *professedly* to be fulfilled and judged of by few. Here, again, come in those unpleasant assertions of the founders of Christianity: " None can say that Jesus is the Lord but by the Holy Ghost." " Do my commandments and ye shall know of the doctrine," etc., etc.—*i.e.* the experiment is *professedly* to be made only with great difficulty and self-denial, and its results can be judged only by a spirit or sense which is only attainable, or which is, at least, only attained, by a few.

The conclusion is this, then, that even if Christianity—as I do not assert—has not sensibly affected "progress," or has affected it as much for the worse in some directions as for the better in others, and has not even done much individual good, in more than a very small proportion, even of those who call themselves Christians; it has only not done what it never professed to do. But has it done what it actually professed to do? That is a question of which the affirmative might be difficult of absolute and generally intelligible *proof*, but of which the negative must, I apprehend, be considered absurd, even by the great majority of those who have never dreamed of qualifying themselves to become final judges of such matters.

There are many passages in Scripture which will readily occur to every reader as being on the surface in contradiction to this limitation by our Lord's own words of the primary purpose of Christianity; but those who know how orphaned and widowed of truth even the best of us are, and how the destitution we may discover in ourselves is greater than that we can know of in any others, will discern, with the earlier and deeper interpreters of the words of our Lord and His Apostles, that there are two ways of reading their exhortations to help the poor, and the declaration that to visit the orphan and the widow is "pure religion and undefiled"; and they will understand that neighbourly service, which is usually (but not always) an inseparable accidental duty of Christian life, is very far indeed from being of primary consequence, though the rendering or not rendering of it—where there is no knowledge of a nobler service—may seriously affect the shallow heavens and the shallow hells of the feebly good and the feebly wicked. Let not such as these exalt themselves against the great Masters of the experimental science of Life, one of whom—St. Theresa, if I remember rightly

—declares that more good is done by one minute of reciprocal contemplative communion of love with God than by the founding of fifty hospitals or of fifty churches. "The elect soul," says another great experimentalist, St. Francis of Sales, "is a beautiful and beloved lady, of whom God demands not the indignity of service, but desires only her society and her person."

IX

A "PESSIMIST" OUTLOOK

DESPOTISM, which is not government, but anarchy speaking with one voice, whether it be the mandate of an irresponsible emperor or that of a multitude, is the "natural" death of all nationalities. They may die by other means, but this is the end they come to if left to themselves. When this end is reached, the corrupt body may, for a time, preserve a semblance of its old identity; but it is no longer a nation: it is merely a localisation of "man's shameful swarm," in which the individual has no help from the infinitely greater and nobler vitality of which he was a living member to erect himself above himself, and to breathe the generous breath, and feel himself in all his acts a partaker of the deceased giant's superhuman vigour. The incidence of the misery is not only upon those comparatively few who may be conscious of its cause. The malaria of the universal marsh stupefies the brain and deadens the heart of the very ploughman who turns its sod, and he is hourly the worse for want of the healthy breeze and invigorating prospect of the ancient hills, which he himself was, perhaps, among the most eager to level. Though he knew it not, he was every day sensibly the better for being the member of a great nation.

> "He felt the giant's heat,
> Albeit he simply called it his,
> Flush in his common labour with delight,
> And not a village maiden's kiss
> But was for this
> More sweet.
> And not a sorrow but did lightlier sigh,
> And for its private self less greet,
> The while that other so majestic self stood by."

If he does not feel the loss of his corporate life, but is content to struggle, stink, and sting with the rest of the swarm into which the national body has been resolved by corruption, so much the worse for him. His insensibility is the perfection of his misery. To others, not so lost, there may be hope, though not in this stage of being. None who has ever lived through the final change, or who, being in the foul morass of resulting "equality," has been able to discern what national life means, can find in private fortune—wife, children, friends, money—any compensation for the great life of which his veins are empty. He knows that there is no proximate hope, no possibility of improvement in such a state of things. He knows that it is absurd to expect anything from "education" of the mass. True education cannot exist under either kind of despotism. National life is the beginning and end of individual culture, as far as this world is concerned. The acquisition of knowledge by an unorganised or enslaved multitude, which must always be, in the main, self-seeking and unjust, is merely the acquisition of subtler and baser means for the advancement of individual covetousness and the indulgence of individual vices. Such education is but "a jewel in a swine's snout." Fools may fill the air with sentimental or hypocritical "aspirations" for the good of the community; but no community exists where no excellence has the power of asserting itself politically, and more or less in spite of the ignorance and malice of those whom it would serve. Such "aspirations" are but the iridescent colours on the stagnant pool; putrid splendours which have no existence in the chronic and salutary storm of national life.

Nor is there any hope from without. A comparatively savage people has often been impregnated with the germ of national being by the military invasion of a civilisation still in the vigour of growth; but there is no instance of a civilisation which has thus lapsed into anarchy having been regenerated by any such means, though its stagnated life may have been perpetuated, as in the case of China, by an external tyranny more powerful than any of the shifting forms of despotism which it develops, if left to itself, from within. Nor is there any light, even in the far future, unless for him who has a fulness of that cosmopolitan benevolence which is so often the boast of the simpleton or the political hypocrite, but, happily, so seldom the possession of the natural man. He knows that no soil has ever yet been found to bear two crops of national life, though the corruption of one has often been found, after many generations of consummated decay, to be very useful dung for the nourishment of other and far·removed fields. But this consideration does not bring him within measurable distance of practical political consolation.

The frantic ambition of one bad man, and the cowardice of half a dozen others, who would have been honest had it not appeared too personally inconvenient, and the apathy of that large portion of the community which has been sane in judgment but insane in sloth, have brought the final evil upon us fifty or a hundred years sooner than it need have come. But come it must have done, sooner or later, since the powers of evil have invariably in worldly matters proved too strong in the long run for those of good; and such as cannot bear this truth, but require that abiding temporal good should come of their good works, had better go into monasteries. Considering what men are, the wonder is, not that all great nationalities should have come to a shameful end, but that their ordinary duration of life should have been a thousand years. How any of them should have lasted a hundred must seem a miracle to those who fail to take into account the agency of the two guardian angels of national life, religion and war—religion which keeps alive the humility and generosity of reasonable submission to law and the spirit of self-sacrifice for corporate life, and war, which silences for a time the envy and hatred of the evil and ignorant for moral and circumstantial superiorities, and compels them to trust their established leaders, on pain of prompt annihilation.

Even our great "liberal" prophet, Mr. Herbert Spencer, is compelled, in spite of himself, to prophesy with terror of what he rightly calls "the coming slavery," the despotism, not of a single irresponsible tyrant, who must content himself with doing good or evil in so general a way that the sense of private compulsion or injury would weigh little on each individual, but the paltry and prying despotism of the vestry—the more "virtuous" the more paltry and prying—persecuting each individual by the intrusion of its myriad-handed, shifting, ignorant, and irresistible tyranny into the regulation of our labour, our household, and our very victuals, and, however "pure" in its abstract intention, necessarily corrupt in its application by its agents, since men, as a rule, are corrupt. Indications are not wanting of the sort of "government" we are committed to, unless the coming war shall leave us in the grip of a less irksome tyranny. It will be a despotism which will have to be mitigated by continual "tips," as the other kind has had to be by occasional assassination. Neither the voter nor the inspector yet know their power and opportunities; but they soon will. We shall have to "square" the district surveyor once or twice a year, lest imaginary drains become a greater terror than real typhoid; we shall have to smoke our pipes secretly and with a sense of sin, lest the moral supervisor of the parish should decline our offer of half-a-crown for holding his nose during his weekly examination of our bedrooms and closets; the good Churchman will have to receive Communion under the "species" of ginger-ale—as some advanced congregations have already proposed—unless the parson can elude the churchwarden with white port, or otherwise persuade him; and, every now and then, all this will be changed, and we shall have to tip our policemen and inspectors for looking over our infractions of popular moralities of a newer pattern. Our condition will very much resemble Swedenborg's hell, in which everbody is incessantly engaged in the endeavour to make everbody else virtuous; and the only compensating comforts to the sane will be that, though wine and tobacco, those natural stimulants to good impulses and fruitful meditations, may be denied him, he may find abundant time and opportunity, in the cessation of all external interests of a moral and intellectual nature, for improving his own character, which, perhaps, is, after all, the only way in which a man can be sure of improving the world's; and, furthermore, he will no longer be discomposed by the prospect of "national disaster," since there can be no national disaster where there is no nation, however freely the gutters may run with blood. Private disaster, in such an infernal millennium, will be a trifle.

Under such conditions, secret societies of discontented and hopeless minorities will abound. Dynamite will often shake the nerves of smug content, and enrage the People beyond bounds at such revolt against its infallible decrees. But none of these societies will be so hateful as the secret and inevitable aristocracy of the remnant that refuses to give interior assent to the divinity of the Brummagen Baal. Its members will acquire means of association and methods of forbidden intrusion which will infuriate the rest, who, in their turn, will invent tests for the discovery, in order to the punishment, of these "enemies of mankind," as the Dutch traders in Japan did, in inviting all persons of doubtful character to trample on the crucifix.

I have called these glances at the near future "pessimist," because that is the word now generally applied to all such forecasts as are made by those who do not ignore or pervert patent facts. "Optimists," as far as I can gather, are those who hope all things from "local option."

X

A SPANISH NOVELETTE

MR. GOSSE is doing useful work in editing a series of translations of remarkable foreign novels, most of which are little known to English readers. To persons—the most of us—whose knowledge of Spanish books is confined to *Don Quixote*, *Pepita Jiménez* will come as a complete and delightful surprise; and yet it not only is, as Mr. Gosse says, "the typical Spanish novel of our days," but it is typical of a great and altogether unique national literature. Though Juan Valera's personality differs from the priestly character of Calderon as far as may well be, since he is said to have made himself "conspicuous by his *bonnes fortunes*, his wild freaks at the gaming-table, his crazy escapades, his feats of horsemanship, and his powers as a toreador," the very same distinguishing vein which makes such plays as Calderon's *Life is a Dream*, and *The Wonder-working Magician* the astonishment and delight of every reader who comes upon them for the first time—an astonishment and delight almost like that of the acquisition of a new sense —this very same vein sparkles through and vivifies the modern novel *Pepita Jiménez*. Alike in Calderon and in this work of Juan Valera we find that complete synthesis of gravity of matter and gaiety of manner which is the glittering crown of art, and which out of Spanish literature is to be found only in Shakespeare, and even in him in a far less obvious degree. It is only in Spanish literature, with the one exception of Dante, that religion and art are discovered to be not necessarily hostile powers; and it is in Spanish literature only, and without any exception, that gaiety of life is made to appear as being not only compatible with, but the very flower of that root which in the best works of other literatures hides itself in the earth, and only sends its concealed sap through stem and leaf of human duty and desire. The reason of this great and admirable singularity seems mainly to have been the singular aspect of most of the best Spanish minds towards religion. With them, religion has been, as it was meant to be, a human passion; they have regarded dogma as the form of realisable, and, by them, realised experience; and the natural instincts of humanity as the outlines of the lineaments of the Divinity—

"very God and very man." Witness the writings of their greatest Saints and theologians, in which dogma is, as it was, fused in, and becomes psychology, instead of remaining, as it has done with us, a rock, indeed, of refuge to many, but a rock of stumbling and offence to many more, and of these especially such as have been endowed with the artistic temperament.

Pepita Jiménez is essentially a "religious novel," none the less so because it represents the failure of a good young aspirant to the priesthood to attain a degree of sanctity to which he was not called, and depicts the working in his aspirations of a pride so subtle as to be very venial, though, in some degree, disastrous. Mr. Gosse seems to me to mistake the *motif* of the novel entirely in regarding it as representing the *necessary* failure of a "divine ardour brought face to face with an earthly love." It represents nothing but the exceedingly common mistake of young and ardent minds in measuring their present capacity by their desires, and striving to take their station on the top of an alp, when they are only fit for the ascent of a very moderate hill. One of the many points in which Catholic philosophy shows itself superior to the philosophy of Protestant religionists in the knowledge of the human mind is its distinct recognition of the fact that there are as many degrees of human capacity for holiness as for any other kind of eminence, and that for most men a very moderate degree of spirituality is the utmost for which they are entitled to hope. An ardent Protestant, misinterpreting the words, " Be ye perfect as I am perfect," is apt to think that he is nothing if not a Saint, whereas Juan Valera knew that to be a Saint, as to be a poet, is to be about one in twenty millions, and he has made a very amusing as well as a very useful book out of the vain strivings of his hero for—

"Heroic good, target for which the young
 Dream in their dreams that every bow is strung;"

and the course of experience by which he is brought to conclude—

"That less than highest is good, and may be high."

That disgusting abortion, the English "religious novel," would have made the enthusiastic young deacon relapse into despair and profligacy, instead of letting him marry the pretty girl who had turned him from his supposed "vocation," and caused him to live an exemplary, conscientious, and religious life as a country gentleman, and farmer of his own land.

There is plenty of "analysis" in the English religious novel, but no psychology; and analysis which has not pyschological knowledge for its material is merely the anatomy of a corpse, and fails as completely in illustrating and extending knowledge of life as the anatomy of the body has confessedly failed, from the time of Galen and Hippocrates, in explaining the vivifying powers of nature. Psychology comes naturally to the typical Spanish mind, for the reasons given above. It deals with the personal relationships of the soul with the personalities which are above the soul, from which the soul exists, and of which the soul is the express mirror; but of these personal relationships, which every religion confesses, the modern mind, out of Spain, *knows* comparatively little, though, thanks to the works of St. John of the Cross (two editions of which have lately appeared in England), and of certain other works, magnificent as literature as well as for burning psychological insight, the study of true psychology, vulgarly called "mysticism" and "transcendentalism" (what good thing is not "mystic" and "transcendental" to the modern "scientist" and his pupils?), shows signs of revival in Europe generally.

A most important consequence of the human character of Spanish faith, a character manifest alike in the religious philosophy of the times of Calderon and of those of Juan Valera, is the utter absence of the deadly Manicheism, which is the source of modern "nicety" in that portion of literature and art which does not profess, like French, and, in great part, American literature and art, to have abandoned all faith and real decency. Calderon, in works which glitter with an incomparable purity, is more plain-spoken, when need be, than Shakespeare, and constantly exalts the splendour of that purity in his main theme by a by-play of inferior characters which is as gay and "coarse" as anything in *Othello* or *Romeo and Juliet;* and though Juan Valera in this novel conforms in the main to the daintiness of the fashion, there is a freedom in his story from the cant of Manichean purity which will certainly limit the number of his readers among ourselves, and probably give some scandal to the most "serious" among those—the immense majority of our countrymen and women—who do not really believe that God made all things pure, and that impurity is nothing but the abuse of that which is pure, and that such abuse is impure in proportion to the purity perverted.

In consequence of the characteristics I have endeavoured to indicate, this novel, though expressly "religious" in its main theme and most of its details, is as "natural," concrete, and wholesomely human and humanly interesting as one of Sir Walter Scott's. There is in it no sense of dislocation or incompatibility between the natural and the spiritual. From the dainty, naïve, innocently coquettish, and passionate Pepita, who is enraged by her lover's pretensions to a piety which, though she is devoted to her beautifully adorned "Infant Jesus," she cannot understand, and in which she sees only an obstacle to the fulfilment of her love for him, to the saintly ecclesiastic, who, almost from the first, sees the incapacity of his pupil, Don Luis, for the celibate heights to which he aspires, but who understands life in all its grades too well to look upon his strivings and his "fall," as Don Luis at first esteems it, with other than a good-humoured smile, all is upon one easy ascending plane and has an intelligible unity. Valera has taken no less care with and interest in the subordinate characters than the principals in the story. They are all true and vivid and unique in their several ways, and we have the most complete picture of a very foreign world without the slightest drawback of strangeness or want of verisimilitude.

XI

BAD MORALITY IS BAD ART

BAD morality is not a necessary condition of good art; on the contrary, bad morality is necessarily bad art, for art is human, but immorality inhuman. The "art" of the present generation is in great part more immoral than any that has preceded it in England. Modern English readers tolerate any amount of corruption, provided only the terms in which it is suggested be not "coarse"; and novels and poems are read, understood, and talked about by young ladies which Rochester would have blushed to be found reading, and which Swift would have called indecent. The delicate indecency of so much modern art is partly due to deficiency of virility, which, in proportion to its strength, is naturally modest. Indecency is an endeavour to irritate sensations and appetites in the absence of natural passion, and that which passes with so many for power and ardour is really impotence and coldness. On the other hand, the ban which these emasculate times have set upon plain-speaking would alone be well-nigh fatal to great art, even were there no other hindrances to it. The loss by the poet of the privilege of plain speaking is equivalent to the loss of the string which Hermes added to Apollo's lute. A whole octave has been withdrawn from the means of expression. Take a single example. Perhaps two or three of Iago's speeches are "coarser" than anything else in English poetry—there is nothing more so in the Bible itself; but the splendour, purity, and solidity of the most splendid, pure, and solid of all dramas that were ever written, depend in very large measure on the way in which these qualities are heightened by those very passages.

For a good many years past the worth of the philosopher and poet has been measured by the width of his departure from the fundamental truth of humanity. But the orthodox truth of humanity is a perennially young and beautiful maiden, whose clothes, however, are liable to get out of fashion, and to bring upon her the appellation of "old frump" from those who are over-anxious to keep up with the *Zeitgeist*. The worthiest occupation of the true poet and philosopher in these days is to provide her with such new clothes as shall make her timely acceptable; and happy is he who shall be found to have contributed even a ribbon or two towards the renovation of her wardrobe, which has of late years fallen so lamentably into decay.

The poet, as a rule, should avoid religion altogether as a direct subject. *Law*, the rectitude of humanity, should be his only subject, as, from time immemorial, it has been the subject of true art, though many a true artist has done the Muse's will and knew it not. As all the music of verse arises, not from infraction, but inflection of the law of the set metre; so the greatest poets have been those the *modulus* of whose verse has been most variously and delicately inflected, in correspondence with feelings and passions which are the inflections of moral law in their theme. Masculine law is always, however obscurely, the theme of the true poet; the feeling and its correspondent rhythm, its feminine inflection, without which the law has no sensitive or poetic life. Art is thus constituted because it is the constitution of life, all the grace and sweetness of which arise from inflection of law, not from infraction of it, as bad men and bad poets fancy.

Law puts a strain upon feeling and feeling responds with a strain upon law, but only such a strain as that with which the hand draws the music from the strings of the lyre. Furthermore, Aristotle says that the quality of poetic language is a continual *slight* novelty. It must needs be so, if poetry would perfectly express poetic feeling, which has also a continual slight novelty, being never alike in any two persons, or on any two occasions. In the highest poetry, like that of Milton, these three modes of inflection, metrical, linguistical, and moral, all chime together in praise of the true order of human life, or moral law. Where this is not recognised there is no good art. What are inflections when there is nothing to inflect? You may get the wail of the Æolian harp, but not music.

Are those great poets wrong, then—the great dramatic poets, especially—whose works abound with representations of infraction of law and its consequent disasters? No. But there are two kinds of inflection and infraction of law: first, of the inner law, which is inflected when a man feels disposed to covet his neighbour's wife and does not, and infracted when he does; secondly, of the outer and vaster law of God's universal justice, which cannot be infracted, but only inflected, even by sin and disaster; the law by which the man shall find it good that he has not followed his natural inclinations, and that by which the man who has so done shall be effectually convinced that the game was not worth the candle. It must be confessed that a large portion of the writings of the very best poets of the past and passing generation has been not art at all, since the one real theme of art has been absent. But it was not thus that Æschylus, Dante, Calderon, and Shakespeare understood "art."

The old commonplace that "Art is essentially religious" is so far true as that the true order of human life is the command, and in part the revelation, of God; but all direct allusion to Him may be as completely omitted as it is from the teaching of the Board School, and yet the art may remain "essentially religious." But the mere *intention* of the artist is not enough to make it so. When Homer and Milton invoked the Muse they meant a reality. They asked for supernatural "*grace*," whereby they might interpret life and nature.

"By grace divine, not otherwise, O Nature, are we thine," says Wordsworth. This gift, without which none can be a poet, is essentially the same thing as that which makes the Saint. Only art is a superficies and life a solid; and the degree of grace which is enough to make a superficies divinely good and beautiful, may leave the solid unaffected. As we all know, a man may be a very good poet, and very little indeed of a Saint. Therefore, I trust that I shall not offend the shade of Shelley, and such of his living successors as feel Shelley's abhorrence of "men who pray," if I say that, notwithstanding their heretical notions of what art should be, there are passages in the works of some of them which distinctly prove that, while writing thus, they were "under the influence of divine grace," of that supernatural spirit without which Nature is not really natural. It is to such passages, and such only, that they owe their claim to be called poets, not to those in which they have ignored or outraged law.

In the very greatest poets, the standard of human law has been absolute sanctity. The keynote of this their theme is usually sounded by them with the utmost reserve and delicacy, especially by Shakespeare, but it is there; and every poet—the natural faculties of the poet being presupposed—will be great in proportion to the strictness with which, in his moral ideal, he follows the counsels of perfection.

XII

EMOTIONAL ART

ONE of the most accomplished writers of the day, a Cambridge lecturer upon poetry, and himself no mean proficient in the art, speaks of poetry as "an art which appeals to the emotions and the emotions only." To what a pass have psychology and criticism come! Poetry, the supreme and peculiar vocation of man, an art in which no woman has attained even the second degree of excellence, to be stigmatised, and that without any intention of affront, as essentially and absolutely feminine! Poetry, in common with, but above all the arts, is the mind of *man*, the rational soul, using the female or sensitive soul, as its accidental or complementary means of expression; persuasive music assisting commanding truth to convince—not God's chosen, to whom truth is its own evidence and its own music—but the Gentiles, to whom pure truth is bitter as hyssop, until, on the lips of the poet, they find it to be sweeter than honey. "The sweetness of the lips increaseth learning." But what is the sweetness of the lips without learning? An alluring harlot, and Mr. Gosse's conception of the Muse! And, alas, not his only, but mainly that of the time, as far as it has any clear conceptions about art at all. Music, painting, poetry, all aspire to be praised as harlots, makers of appeals "to the emotions and the emotions only." Art, indeed, works most frequently and most fruitfully *through* such appeals; but so far is such appeal from being its essence, that art, universally acknowledged to be of the very highest kind, sometimes almost entirely dispenses with "emotion," and trusts for its effect to an almost purely intellectual expression of form or order—in other words, of truth; for truth and order are one, and the music of Handel, the poetry of Æschylus, and the architecture of the Parthenon are appeals to a sublime good sense which takes scarcely any account of "the emotions."

But far be it from me to undervalue the emotions, by a due expression of which the "poet sage" becomes indeed the apostle of the Gentiles; and by giving to which, in his life and work, their due place, he becomes in soul and act what man was made to be, namely, the image of God, who is described in the Orphic hymn as "a beautiful youth and a divine nymph." In proportion as a man, above all a poet, has in his constitution the "divine nymph," the "sensitive soul," so is the "beautiful youth," the "rational mind," great in its influential force; provided that the masculine character holds itself always supreme over the feminine, which is really only in so far sweet as it is in subordination and obedience. I may go further, and say that no art can appeal "to the emotions only" with the faintest hope of even the base success it aspires to. The pathos of such art (and pathos is its great point) is wholly due to a more or less vivid expression of a vague remorse at its divorce from truth and order. The Dame aux Camélias sighs in all Chopin's music over her lost virtue, which, however, she shows no anxiety to recover, and the characteristic expression of the most recent and popular school of poetry and painting is a ray of the same sickly and in the most part hypocritical homage to virtue. Without some such homage, even the dying and super-sensitive body of "emotional" art loses the very faintest pretensions to the name of art, and becomes the confessed carrion of Offenbach's operas and the music hall. Atheism in art, as well as in life, has only to be pressed to its last consequences in order to become ridiculous, no less than disastrous; and the "ideal," in the absence of an idea or intellectual reality, becomes the "realism" of the brothel and the shambles.

The advocate of art for "the emotions and the emotions only," cannot be brought to understand that the alternative is not "didactic" art, which is as much a contradiction in terms as his own notion of art is. Of great and beautiful things beauty and greatness are the only proofs and expressions; and the ideas of the greatest artists are the morality of a sphere too pure and high for "didactic" teaching. The teaching of art is the suggestion—far more convincing than assertion—of an ethical science, the germs of which are to the mass of mankind incommunicable; and the broad daylight of this teaching can be diffused only by those who live in and absorb the direct splendour of an unknown, and, to the generality, an unknowable sun. The mere ignoring of morality, which is what the more respectable of modern artists profess, will not lift them into the region of such teachers; much less will the denial of morality do so, as some modern artists seem to think. The Decalogue is not art, but it is the guide-post which points direct to where the source of art springs; and it is now, as in the day when Numa and Moses made their laws:—he is profane who presents to the gods the fruit of an unpruned vine; that is, sensitive worship before the sensitive soul has been sanctified by habitual confession of and obedience to the rational; and still worse than he who offers the Muses the "false fire" of his gross senses is he who heats the flesh-pots of Egypt with flames from the altar, and renders emotions, which were intended to make the mortal immortal, themselves the means and the subjects of corruption. Of all kinds of corruption, says St. Francis of Sales, the most malodorous is rotten lilies.

By very far the largest proportion of "the emotions," namely, corporeal pleasures and pains, have no place at all in true art, unless, indeed, they may be occasionally and sparingly used as *discords* in the great harmony of the drama. Joy, and pathos of its privation, are the "pain" and "pleasure" of art, poetic "melancholy" and "indignation" being the sigh of joy indefinitely delayed, and wroth at the obstruction of its good by evil. These form the main region of the lyric poet. But, as joy and pathos are higher than pleasure and pain, being concerned with the possession or privation of a real good, so in *peace*, which is as much above joy as joy is above pleasure, and which can scarcely be called emotion, since it rests, as it were, in final good, the *primum mobile*, which is without motion—we find ourselves in the region of "great" art. Pleasure is an itch of the cold and corrupt flesh, and must end with corruption; joy is the life of the natural and innocent breast, prophesying peace, but too full of desire to obtain it yet; peace is the indwelling of God and the habitual possession of all our desires, and it is too grave and quiet even for a smile.

This character of peace in art and life has sometimes affected entire states of civilisation, hovering like an angel even in atmospheres profoundly tainted with impurities, and giving an involuntary greatness to the lives and works of men to whom its source was invisible; breathing through the veils of Eleusis the beauty of the glorified body into the marbles of Phidias, and guiding the brush of Titian and Raphael, and even the chisel of Cellini, by the hand of a spirit whose dwelling was the inmost sanctuary of the Temple.

What then, it will be answered, shall be said of that poetry, some of it the most exquisite in the world, which seeks only to evoke an echo, in the reader's bosom, of human love? This: That love—if it be worthy of the name—is the highest of virtues, as well as the sweetest of emotions. Nay, that it is the sweetest of emotions because it is the highest of virtues, ordering the whole being of man "strongly and sweetly"; being in the brain confession of good; in the heart, love of, and desire to sacrifice everything for the good of its object; in the senses, peace, purity, and ardour.

XIII

PEACE IN LIFE AND ART

IF we compare ancient with modern art, and the minds and manners of our far ancestors with the minds and manners of the present time, it can hardly fail to strike us that the predominant presence of peace in the former and its absence in the latter constitute the most characteristic difference. Peace, as it was held to be the last effect and reward of a faithful life, was regarded as the ideal expression of life in painting, sculpture, poetry, and architecture; and accordingly the tranquil sphere of all the greatest of great art is scarcely troubled by a tear or a smile. This peace is no negative quality. It does not consist in the mere absence of disturbance by pain or pleasure. It is the peace of which St. Thomas says " perfect joy and peace are identical," and is the atmosphere of a region in which smiles and tears are alike impertinences. In such art the expression of pain and pleasure is never an end, as it almost always is with us moderns, but a means of glorifying that peace which is capable of supporting either without perturbation. "Peace," says again the great writer above quoted, "is the tranquillity of order, and has its seat in the will." A word about this living order, which all great art aspires to express. Each soul is created to become a beauty and felicity which is in a measure unique, and every one who has attained to a life upon his own lines desires to become more and more truly and manifestly this singular excellence and happiness for which he alone was born. This is his "ruling love," his individuality, the centre towards which his thoughts and actions gravitate, and about which his whole being revolves; while this individual being again travels about that greater centre which gives a common unity and generosity to all individualities. This double order has its exact analogue in that of the motions of the heavenly bodies, and is that by which alone the motions of souls are made heavenly. For the proof of this doctrine no one need go further than his conscience—if he has one. If he has not, since there is no peace for the like of him, the discussion of its nature need not occupy his attention.

This peace, which is the common character of

all true art and of all true life, involves, in its fullest perfection, at once the complete subdual and the glorification of the senses, and the "ordering of all things strongly and sweetly from end to end."

> "Forth from the glittering spirit's peace
> And gaiety ineffable
> Streams to the heart delight and ease,
> As from an overflowing well;
> And, orderly deriving thence
> Its pleasure perfect and allow'd,
> Bright with the spirit shines the sense,
> As with the sun a fleecy cloud."

It is sufficient, however, for the honour of art and life that peace should be dominant in the mind and will. Lessing observes that the dignity and repose of Greek tragedy is in no way disturbed by cries of grief and pain, too violent for modern art, because the tragedian makes it clear that these perturbations are only in the outer man, the stability of the interior being therefore illustrated rather than clouded by such demonstrations. In the Shakspearian tragedy the seat of this supreme expression is removed, for the most part, from the personality of the characters engaged, to the mind of the reader, reflecting that of the poet, who evolves peace from the conflict of interests and passions to which the predominance and victory of a single moral idea gives unity. That idea is never embodied in any single conspicuous character, though it is usually allowed an unobtrusive expression in some subordinate personality, in order to afford a clue to the "theme" of the whole harmony. Such theme-suggesting characters are, for example, the Friar in *Romeo and Juliet*, and Kent in *King Lear*, who represent and embody the law from which all the other characters depart more or less, with proportionate disaster to themselves.

Delights and pleasures demand, no less than grief and pain, to be subordinated to peace, in order to become worthy of life and art. The cynicism and the corrupt melancholy of much of our modern life and art are the inevitable results of the desires being set upon delights and pleasures in which there is not peace.

The peace, which is "identical with perfect joy" in life and its expression in art, is also identical with purity, which is so far from being, as is commonly supposed, a negative quality, that it is the unimpeded ardour of ordered life in all its degrees, and is as necessary to the full delight of the senses as it is to the highest felicity of the spirit. Hence the greatest art, in which all things are "ordered sweetly" by essential peace, and in which pleasure is only the inevitable accident, is exceedingly bold.

Its thoughts are naked and not ashamed; and Botticelli, in his celestial "Venus" in the National Gallery, expresses, without raising a disorderly fancy, things which Titian, in his leering Venus of the stews, at Florence, is too "chaste" to hint.

There are, probably, few persons who are so unhappy as not to have experienced a few moments in life during which they they have drawn breath in a region in which pleasure and pain are discerned to be, in themselves, neither good nor evil, and even so much like each other that there is not much to choose between them. Those who have known such moments, and who preserve the memory of them as the standard of life, at least in desire, have alone the key to the comprehension of great art, or the possibility of approaching to it in execution. Such knowledge so respected is the initial condition of that alone true "style" which is the unique aspect of the individual soul to the absolute beauty and joy; of that living "repose, which marks the manners of the great" in art, and which bears upon the stately movement of its eternal stream the passions, pains, and pleasures of life like eddies which show the motion that is too great to be perturbed by them.

For the time, at least, this quality, as I have said, has almost disappeared from art. It lingered in the best poetry, painting, and music of the last century and of the beginning of this. It was the ideal to which Goethe, Coleridge, Keats, and Wordsworth aspired, and in a few pieces attained. The gravity of Handel is sweet with it, and the sweetness of Mozart grave. Gainsborough, Crome, and Hogarth were moved by it, more or less; and we still judge art—such of us as have any power of judgment—by the standard of this glory, though we have lost the secret of its creation.

XIV

SIMPLICITY

THERE are three simplicities; that of the child, "On whom those truths do rest which we are toiling all our lives to find"; the simplicity of genius; and the simplicity of wisdom. "The single eye, which makes the body full of light"—in modern phrase, the synthetical faculty and habit—is the essential character of all simplicity, and it is never separated from a certain innocence and *naïveté;* and quiescence or perfection of conscience appear to be its conditions. The paradisaical, or synthetic, vision in the child is conditioned by the innocence of ignorance and its inevitable freedom from the habit of analysis; the mind of the child goes forth into particulars with a congenital discernment of the living unity of which the child itself is, as yet, a part; and it continues so to go forth until it falls into some disorder of will or understanding or both, which is separation from that unity, and extinction of "the single eye." Genius consists wholly in the possession of the divine faculty of synthetic or unitive apprehension, in maturer years, and in company with consciousness or the power of reflection. This possession is so exceedingly rare, whole nations and generations having existed without producing a single noticeable instance of it, that it must be regarded, not as the natural culmination of humanity, but as a splendid and fortunate anomaly, or departure from the law of the race. In some few of the very few, indeed, it seems to have been in natural order, the simplicity and purity of childhood having been retained and developed through life, until it has become the simplicity of wisdom; but no one who has made himself acquainted with the lives of men of genius can fail to have observed that a concomitant of their wonderful privilege has usually been a certain dislocation and startling disproportion in faculty and character. Simplicity or *naïveté*, as Lessing remarks, has invariably more or less characterised them and their work; but, in most instances they seem, if one may say so, to have had no moral right to this singular grace, and even sometimes to have preserved or attained it by bold denial or by mere oblivion of its natural conditions—an oblivion not unfrequently amounting to moral insanity. It has, in such cases, been like the precious gum, or profuse flush of flower, which comes of disease in the tree. The three constituent parts of man, the intellect, will, and perception, in such cases, do not act together, as they do in healthy persons, but the exorbitancy of perception seems to be the result of a lethargy of intellect and will which leaves the whole energy of life to go forth into perception, as it does in the child through like conditions, conditions which in the child, however, are the right order of its being. The past century, which has been so extraordinarily productive of men of genius, has produced a more than usual proportion of those in whom genius has been the concomitant of mental and moral defect and disorder. The works of such men are marked by exceeding inequality, deserts of dulness as in Coleridge, or of mere imbecility as in Blake, occasionally and suddenly blossoming as the rose, or the intermittent flush of beauty and fictitious health in the face of one dying of decline.

There is another kind of simplicity, which is endowed, like the others, with the synthetic eye, and which is the only kind that is of much abiding value to its possessor; namely, the simplicity of wisdom. This is rarely found except in persons of advanced years. The simplicity of age is the blossom of which that of childhood is the bud and almost always failing promise. Its great condition is innocence, which has been retained through or recovered during the struggles and temptations of manhood; and, as the innocence of knowledge is far nobler than that of infantine ignorance, so its reward, the unitive vision, has an immeasurably wider field. Such men, at seventy, see again the daisy as they saw it when they were seven; but a universe of realities, unknown in childhood, is discerned by them as a single flower of which each particular reality is a petal; and the life-long unconscious analysis, which has been to other men corruption, has only provided them with a vaster prospect of the elemental integrity, and an inexhaustible source of joy, which, like that of the "young-eyed cherubim," is too grave for smiles.

XV

ANCIENT AND MODERN IDEAS OF PURITY

FEW persons who are not scholars have any knowledge of the difference which there is between ancient and modern ideas of purity, and few moralists have considered or admitted how very largely the comparison, if fairly made, must tell in favour of the ancients, who may be reckoned, in this matter, to have ceased about the time of the Reformation. As it was impurity which first brought fig-leaves into fashion, so the wonderful and altogether unprecedented addiction to that fashion, during the past three hundred years, may be taken as a fair measure of what puritanism has done, during that period, for us, and is still doing, —still doing, for, within the last few years, the actual fig-leaf has invaded the Vatican itself; and even there we are no longer allowed to contemplate "the human form divine," unprofaned by reminders of the niceness of nasty thinkers.

If we go back to those first ages of Christianity—which modern good people, who know nothing about them, regard with such reverence—we shall find that the greatest and purest of the "Fathers of the Church" were in the practice of addressing their flocks with an outspokenness which is not surpassed even by the ancient expounders of the Eleusinian and Bacchic mysteries, or, for that matter, by the Bible itself. St. Augustine, for example, in the *City of God* and elsewhere, says things fit to throw decent people into convulsions; and nowhere, in ancient Christian writings, do we find ignorance regarded as even a part, much less the whole, of innocence:—witness the words of Her, who is the model of innocence to all ages, in her answer, at thirteen years of age, to the message of Gabriel.

Strange to say, this modern notion of purity is not limited to those Churches which owe their origin to the Reformation. Their spirit has so deeply infected the Mother Church that, though her abstract doctrine remains the same as it was, she practically enforces the negative idea as jealously as it is enforced among good Protestants, or even more jealously, so that the ancient idea of positive purity, as a sacred fire which consumes and turns into its own substance all that is adverse to it, is now substituted by the conception that it is of the nature of stored snow, which must be kept artificially dark and cool, lest it disappear for ever. "Why, papa, I thought that marriage was rather a wicked sacrament!" said a young lady, who had been brought up at one of the best convent schools in England, the other day to her father, when he happened to be praising that institution. And in the great English Catholic Colleges for boys, the wonderful phenomenon may now be seen of two or three hundred lads and young men whose minds, with regard to the relations of the sexes, are exactly in the same condition as those of the girls, and whose only idea of marriage—gathered from the shyness with which the whole subject is avoided by all about them—is, that it is "rather a wicked sacrament." The prolongation of the innocence of ignorance into advanced youth would probably be unmixed gain were it not that knowledge, being left to come by accident, is almost sure to become poisoned in the moment of acquisition. It is of little use calling the legitimate connection of the sexes a "great sacrament," if no pains are taken to identify the knowledge of that connection with the knowledge of what is meant by a sacrament, this latter knowledge being the ground of the immense difference between the pagan and Christian views of marriage, and if the essential sanctity of chastity, married or unmarried, is left to be discovered only by the obscuration of the conscience in its loss. The whole sphere of the doctrines of the early Church, like that of all the great mythologies, revolved about mysteries which the modern Churches, in practice, absolutely ignore, but which nature, however improved by grace, absolutely refuses to ignore. The result is a practical Manicheism, which is as serious in its effects upon morals as it is treasonous to the truth. The prodigious evils of unchastity prove sufficiently that chastity is no merely negative good. *Corruptio optimi pessima.* But where is the safeguard of purity if its corruption is imagined to be the corruption, not of the " best," but of some shadowy and negative state? To avoid this immeasurable evil there should be prudent and bold plain-speaking, on fitting occasions.

Plain-speaking does not vitiate. Even coarseness is health compared with those suppressed forms of the disease of impurity which come of our modern undivine silences.

A young man or woman must be hopelessly corrupt who would be injured by the freest reading of the Bible, or Shakespeare. The most pure and exalted love-poem that was ever written, Spenser's *Epithalamion* on his own marriage, is also one of the most "nude"; and all art-students "from the life" know that it is ingenious dress far more than the absence of dress that has dangerous attractions.

The boldest confession of the doctrine of the Incarnation, with all its corollaries, has been the father of that splendid virtue which was but dimly foreshown in pre-Christian ideas of purity. Whereever this doctrine has been denied or hesitatingly taught, it is a fact of simple experience that chastity has suffered with it. For what considerations can ordinary morals or the widest suggestions of worldly expediency substitute for those with which the New Testament abounds? "Bear and glorify God in your bodies"; "shall I take the members of Christ and make them the members of a harlot?" "God for the body, and the body for God," etc.

XVI

CONSCIENCE

THE twofold constitution of man which, the more it is reflected upon, becomes the more manifest and wonderful, and seems more and more to approach the reality of a double personality in one being—the duality which the old theologians and philosophers recognised in speaking of man's nature as composed of a rational and of a sensitive, or of a male and female soul—is in nothing more obvious to persons who really consider their own business than in the phenomena of conscience. In every person who has a right to be called a person, as distinguished from an animal, there are two distinct consciences: the rational or male conscience, that commands him to act according to certain fixed laws which he knows or believes to be just and right; and the sensitive or female conscience, which persuades, indeed, to apparent good, but which, in default of habitual subordination to the virile conscience, does more harm in the world, although it is a sort of virtue, than is done by any vice. It is full of scruples about small things, and is often indifferent to great. Its chief care is for things present and external. To sympathise with and alleviate present and physical or emotional suffering, and evils often simply fanciful, and to forgive things which ought not to be forgiven, is the extent of its "charity"; and its character, in all but highly disciplined and robust minds, is to be in almost continual conflict with the rational conscience. So that the struggles of a really good man are not so much against evil, which, known to be such, does not attract him, as against the inexpedient good which his inferior conscience is perpetually recommending to him with the most confusing plausibility, and which, if it be not listened to, cries out against him with lamentations and reproaches, often hard to distinguish from the voice of his own proper guide. It is so especially when, as is mostly the case, this female objurgator charges him with refusing to make sacrifices which are not only uncalled for, but would be injurious to his own true welfare and that of others, if they were made. This conflict caused the Apostle to cry out, "The whole creation groaneth together until now, waiting for the manifestation of the sons of God, to wit the redemption of the body"—the "body," the "woman," and the sensitive "soul" being synonyms to his mind as to that of all ancient philosophers. The sons of God—*i.e.* the true and faithful—however perfect in will and deed, cannot be "manifested" while they are thus in opposition to their sensitive life, which should be their helpmate and "glory," instead of their troublesome adversary and accuser. In some exceedingly small proportion of good people this glowing female conscience has been so persistently resisted and ordered by severe and undeviating obedience to "cold" and purely rational dictates, that such persons are not only no longer troubled by the insubordination and contradictions of the sensitive nature, but they find themselves—often suddenly and unexpectedly —in more or less complete harmony and co-operation with her. She has submitted; and the true life, which had been hitherto arduous and full of trouble, is thenceforward full of the joy as well as the power of the Divine Spirit; she having become his "glory," as she was before his accuser and shame, and the means instead of the hinderer of his "manifestation" as a "son of God."

It must be repeated, however, that the inferior conscience is not a vice, but a virtue without sufficient light; and that it is far more likely to call for unnecessary labour and sacrifice and to suggest false and harassing scruples than to invite to ease and self-indulgence. The *false* conscience, by which the mass of men justify to themselves their persistence in ignorance and self-seeking, or brace themselves to the difficult pursuit of unjust ends without regard to law, is a very different thing.

It should be remembered that even the truest conscience is not an illuminating power, though illumination is sure to follow obedience to it. It is a commanding voice, that bids all and compels some to follow their best attainable light ; which being done, there is no sin, though there may be great and temporarily terrible error in such obedience. So much for the individual conscience. Let it be added that when a whole nation comes to be mainly guided by the female or sensitive conscience, so far as it has any conscience at all, then great disaster is not far off.

XVII

ON OBSCURE BOOKS

THE next best thing to understanding an obscure matter, and the first and most necessary step towards understanding it, is to know that you do not understand it, waiving for a time and in your own respect the popular and pleasant assumption that everything in which there is anything to be understood can be understood by everybody and at once. The threadbare saying, "If you do not understand a man's ignorance, you should think yourself ignorant of his understanding," should be cherished by every reader who does not read merely to pass the time. Active, intelligent, and modest minds are able, in most cases, to discover at a glance whether the obscurity of a book is due to the author's ignorance or their own; but, unhappily, such minds are rare; and the consequence is that most of the great books of the world rest unread upon the dusty bookshelves of our big libraries. "What is the use of reading books which, perhaps, we could not understand, if we tried ever so much? And what a bore it would be to learn to understand them if we could," is the remark that will naturally occur. But the fact is that the obscure works of great writers are never wholly obscure, unless they are purely technical and scientific; and that the little which may easily be understood in them is generally sweeter and brighter than all the sweetness and light of many a perfectly intelligible and widely popular author.

Nor is the reading the less pleasant to any one who seeks more in reading than the merest amusement, because the way is somewhat rough, and there may be great boulders or even craggy hills which he must avoid and go round instead of over. The way often sparkles with gems of forgotten novelty, and it is the most agreeable of surprises to find how many problems which agitate the contemporary heart have been settled once and for ever, hundreds or thousands of years ago. You may not understand one-tenth of a treatise by Aristotle, St. Augustine, St. Thomas Aquinas, Swedenborg, or Hegel; but what you do comprehend remains engraved in your memory like a precious intaglio, and you find that you have been learning *things* and not listening to gossip *about* things. Then there is the pleasure—always great to an active mind—of being active. You have to ask yourself at every step whether you have rightly understood; and, whether you concur or not, the novelty of style excites your intelligence, instead of laying it to sleep, as the smooth conventional language of the day often does, so that you think you understand when you do not, or when, perhaps, there has been nothing to understand. Again, the often hopeless obscurities of some passages throw the clearer parts into such splendid clearness! How delightful to find in Plato, among a good deal from which the light has, perhaps, for ever departed, a political passage, long, clear, forcible, and as *à propos* as if it had been written yesterday by a supernaturally vigorous correspondent of the *Times*. Nor is the reading of the authors of great exploded systems of philosophy to be neglected. Though erroneous as well as obscure, the errors of great original thinkers are commonly related in a more living manner to truth than the commonplaces and pretentious *réchauffés* of the present day; and, in the course of proving what may now seem, or may really be, an absurd proposition, they often scatter about them many sparks of living truth, any one of which might suffice for the theme about which a nineteenth-century writer might talk profoundly through sixteen pages of a first-class periodical. Even from a far less elevated point of view than that of the true student, the reading of such books is in its results profitable and delightful. If you want to shine as a diner-out, the best way is to know something which others do not know, and not to know many things which everybody knows. This takes much less reading, and is doubly effective, inasmuch as it makes you a really good, that is, an interested listener, as well as a talker. Your neighbour at the board can tell you what the *Times* or the *Contemporary Review*, which you have not read, says about the matter, and you can supplement the information by something on the subject from Hobbes or Hooker; and each converses with the pleasant sense of being superior to the other, and able to instruct him.

But to return to the point of view of the student, there is no more agreeable result of reading such books as we are treating of than that of gradually discovering that great Doctors of the Church, schoolmen, mystics, and others were not such idiots as we fancied we were bound to believe them to have been, and as, indeed, such elegant extracts as are all that is known of them by most enlightened persons may seem to prove them to have been. Such passages may appear to be not obscure, but very clear nonsense, and may seem to imply, if we know no more, that these writers could not possibly write sensibly on anything. But the result of a direct and considerate acquaintance with their books themselves may be the discovery of quite simple explanations of such seemingly hopeless anomalies; for example, the strange traditional practice which prevailed among the schoolmen, and prevails in some theological schools even in the present day, of confirming a thesis by some brief and quite inconclusive argument or authority, and then going on with the real proof in the body of the chapter or article, is the clue to the existence of many most amusing demonstrations of the imbecility of men who have won immortal names for their learning and sagacity. But perhaps the greatest of all the advantages of this sort of reading is the advantage of keeping company with the intellectually great, apart from any specific and tangible acquisition of knowledge. Great authors are always greater than their books. The best part of the best play of Shakespeare is Shakespeare himself, the vast, wholesome, serene, and unique individuality which stands above and breathes through tragedy and comedy alike. Fortunately, the most ordinary education implies contact with several of these primary spheres of benign influence; but there are many others, totally different in character, which might be approached with the same kind of benefit by the general student, but scarcely ever are. Of course, the principal excuse for this is that many or most such works as we are contemplating are in some language which the ordinary reader—though he may have been at a public school and University—cannot comfortably read. But this excuse is insufficient. The best writers, even the best poets, bear translation best; and unless a man can read Greek comfortably, which is really an exceedingly rare accomplishment, or can peruse Latin freely, which is not at all a common acquirement, even among the most expensively educated, he will get much more of the author's thought by handling fairly good translations than by consulting originals, of which the inherent obscurity may be quite sufficient for his patience.

XVIII

"DISTINCTION"[1]

I HAVE been taken to task at great length and with great severity by the *Spectator* for having identified the "elect" with the "select"; and the *Guardian* has charged me, in terms not less profuse and energetic, with entertaining "flunkey" notions, not only of this life, but of the next. The *Spectator*, furthermore, denounces me as a person of singularly "savage" and "scornful" disposition. Now, as these are moral rather than literary censures, and as any one may, if he likes, consider that he is under obligation to defend his character publicly when it has been publicly impugned, I desire to say a few words in explana-

---

[1] When this Essay appeared in the *Fortnightly Review* it was taken so much *au grand sérieux* by the newspapers, especially the *Spectator*, that I resolved never thenceforward to attempt to deal in "chaff" or fun, without clearly intimating my intention at the outset.

tion of expressions and sentiments which I think that my judges have misinterpreted.

I confess frankly to a general preference for persons of "distinction," and even to believing that they are likely to have a better time of it hereafter than the undistinguished, but I humbly and sincerely protest to my monitors that I do not, as they assume, identify "distinction" with wealth, culture, and modern Conservative politics, though I do hold that in the absence of culture, "distinction" rarely becomes apparent, just as, in the absence of polish, the tints and veins of a fine wood or marble, though they may be there, are little evident. In this world, at least, "de non apparentibus et de non existentibus eadem est ratio."

If we could see the soul of every man—as, indeed, we can, more or less, in his face, which is never much like the face of any other—we should see that every one is in some degree "distinguished." He is born "unique," and does not make himself so, though, by fidelity to himself and by walking steadily and persistently on his own line, his distinction can be indefinitely increased, as it can be indefinitely diminished by the contrary process, until he may end in extinction; for, interiorly, man lives by contrast and harmonious opposition to others, and the communion of men upon earth as of Saints in heaven abhors identity more than nature does a vacuum. Nothing so shocks and repels the living soul as a row of exactly similar things, whether it consists of modern houses or of modern people, and nothing so delights and edifies as "distinction."

It was said of a celebrated female Saint that she did nothing but what was done by everybody else, but that she did all things as no one else did them. In manners and art, as in life, it signifies far less *what* is done or said than *how* it is done and said; for the unique personality, the alone truly interesting and excellent thing, the "distinction," comes out in the latter only.

I am old enough, and have been lucky enough —no doubt, through favour rather than through the manifestation of any distinction of my own— to have been occasionally present at small private gatherings of eminent statesmen and literary men, in times when such eminence usually savoured of distinction; and I confess that I have had few experiences which so helped me to understand how pleasant a thing life might become under supernaturally favourable circumstances.

My friendly monitors of the *Guardian* and *Spectator* may, perhaps, discover further confirmation, in these words, of their impression that I am at once a "flunkey" and a "savage," and my confession may recall to their minds that other savage to whom the missionary sought in vain to convey any idea of Heaven until he compared it with a perpetual feast of buffalo-beef well masticated by a squaw. Well, difference, though it may not amount to distinction, is better than dull uniformity; and I will go on my own way without nourishing ill-will towards my critics, and, I hope, without provoking it in them. There is so little distinction now, that I will not quarrel with anybody for not understanding me when I praise it. In English letters, for example, now that Matthew Arnold and William Barnes are gone, and Dr. Newman and Lord Tennyson are silent, distinction has nearly vanished.

The verse of Mr. William Morris, always masterly, is sometimes really distinguished, as in the prelude and some of the lyrics of *Love is Enough*. The distinction, too, of Mr. Swinburne's writing is occasionally unquestionable; but he allows himself to be troubled about many things, and would, I fancy, write more poetically, if less forcibly, were his patriotism not so feverish, and his horror of the errors and wickedness of Popery more abstract, disinterested, and impersonal. He is wanting, I venture to think, in what Catholic moralists call "holy indifference." Distinction is also manifest in the prose of Mr. George Meredith when the cleverness is not too overwhelming to allow us to think of anything else; but, when the nose of epigram after epigram has no sooner reached the visual nerve than the tail has whisked away from it, so that we have had no time to take in the body, our wonder and bedazement make it sometimes impossible for us to distinguish the distinction, if it be there. Mr. Pater, Mr. Symonds, and Mr. Henley are not without claim to rank with the "quality," though their distinction is a trifle too intentional. Mrs. Meynell, alone, is, both in prose and verse, almost always thoroughly distinguished.

Democracy hates distinction, though it has a humble and pathetic regard for eminence and rank; and eminence and rank, by the way, never paid a more charming and delicate compliment to Democracy than when Lord Rosebery affirmed that the test of true literature, and its only justifiable *Imprimatur*, is "the thumb-mark of the artisan."

The ten or so superior and inexhaustibly fertile periodical writers who (with three or four fairly good novelists) now represent English literature, and are the arbiters and, for the most part, the monopolists of fame, share the dislike of their *clientèle* to "distinction," suppressing it, when it ventures to appear, with a "conspiracy of silence" more effective than the guillotine, while they exalt the merit which they delight to honour by voices more overwhelming than the *plébiscite*. Witness the fate of William Barnes, who, though far from being the deepest or most powerful, was by far the most uniformly "distinguished" poet of our time. Mr. G. S. Venables said, perhaps, no more than the truth when he declared, as he did in my hearing, that there had been no poet of such peculiar perfection since Horace. Mr. F. T. Palgrave has also done him generous and courageous justice. But what effect have these voices had against the solid silence of non-recognition by our actual arbiters of fame? He is never named in the authentic schedules of modern English poets. I do not suppose that any one nearer to a Countess than his friend Mrs. Norton ever asked him to dinner, and there was not so much as an enthusiastic Dean to decree (upon his own respectable responsibility) the national honour of burial in Westminster Abbey to the poor classic. On the other hand, the approving voices of our literary and democratic Council of Ten or so are as tremendously effective as their silence. No such power of rewarding humble excellence ever before existed in the world. Mrs. Lynn Lynton, of her own knowledge, writes thus: "Of a work, lately published, one man alone wrote sixteen reviews.

The author was his friend, and in sixteen 'vehicles' he carried the flag of his friend's triumph." To compare good things with bad, this beneficent ventriloquism reminds one of Milton's description of the devil, in the persons of the priests of Baal, as "a liar in four hundred mouths."

I hope that I may further exonerate myself from the charge of a proclivity to "plush"—this, if I remember rightly, was the word used by the *Guardian*—and also from that of a "savage" disrespect for modern enlightenment, as authenticated by "the thumb-mark of the artisan," when I go on to say that, to my mind, there can be no "distinction," in life, art, or manners, worth speaking of, which is not the outcome of singular courage, integrity, and generosity, and, I need scarcely add, of intellectual vigour, which is usually the companion of those qualities habitually exercised. An accomplished distinction, as the sight of it gives the greatest delight to those who have it, or are on the way to the attainment of it, so it is the greatest of terrors to the vulgar, whether of the gutter or in gilded chambers. Their assertion of their sordid selves it rebukes with a silence or a look of benevolent wonder, which they can never forgive, and which they always take for indications of intolerable pride, though it is nothing other than the fitting and inevitable demeanour, under the circumstances, of the "good man, in whose eyes," King David says, "a vile person is despised"; or that recommended by St. Augustine, who tells us that, if a man does not love the living truth of things, you should "let him be as dirt" to you; or by a still higher Authority, who directs you to treat such an one as a "sinner and a publican," or, in modern phrase, a "cad." Naturally, the average democrat—who has not yet learned to love the living truth of things—resents "distinction," and pathetically turns to Lord Rosebery and other such highly certificated judges of what is really excellent for consolation and reassurance; and naturally the leaders of democracy, in the House of Commons, or in the newspapers and magazines, are as jealous of distinction as the Roman democrats were of the man who presumed to roof his house with a pediment—which, perhaps, reminded them too disagreeably of a Temple.

The finest use of intercourse, whether personal or through books, with the minds of others is not so much to acquire their thoughts, feelings, and characters as to corroborate our own, by compelling these to "take aspect," and to derive fresh consciousness, form, and power to our proper and peculiar selves. Such intercourse not only brings latent "distinction" into life, but it increases it more and more; a beautiful and beloved opposition acting as the scientific toy called the "electric doubler," by which the opposite forces in the two juxtaposed discs may be accumulated almost without limit, and splendid coruscations of contrasting life evoked, where there apparently was mere inertness before. The best use of the supremely useful intercourse of man and woman is not the begetting of children, but the increase of contrasted personal consciousness.

All attraction and life are due to magnetic opposition, and a great individuality, appearing in any company, acts as a thunder-cloud, which brightens the circumjacent air by alluring to or repelling from itself all the dusty and inert particles which float so thickly in the air of ordinary companies. The Catholic Church, whose *forte*, I think, is psychological insight, is peculiarly sensible in this, that, instead of encouraging uniformity of thought and feeling, as all other Churches do, she does her best, in the direction of souls, to develop as wide a distinction as is consistent with formal assent to her singularly few articles of obligatory faith. She requires consent to the letter of the doctrine, but welcomes as many and seemingly conflicting ways of viewing it as there are idiosyncrasies of character in men, recommending each not to force his inclination, but to seek such good in the doctrine as best suits him.

Thus does she encourage the immense diversity with which the final vision of Truth shall be reflected in prismatic glories from the "Communion of the Saints."

In the world, as I have said, distinction can scarcely be manifested without a certain amount of culture, especially that part of culture which consists in simplicity, modesty, and veracity. But culture in the democracy is usually deficient in these characteristics, and is also wanting in that purity of manner and phraseology without which delicate distinctions of nature are, more or less, indecipherable. Plain speaking—sometimes very unpleasantly plain speaking—may be consistent with distinction; but until Sir William Harcourt, Mr. Labouchere, and Mr. Gladstone, for example, learn to leave off calling Tory spades sanguinary shovels, their eminent personalities must lack one fundamental condition of true self-manifestation. Persons who habitually express themselves so loosely must rest content, in this world, with something short of true distinction, though when they shall have attained to the Communion of Saints it may become unexpectedly conspicuous in them. So in art. In poetry, for instance, good and simple manners and language are not distinction, but distinction nowhere appears without them. The ordinary laws of language must be observed, or those small inflections of customary phrase, that "continual slight novelty," which is, as Aristotle, I think, says, the essential character of poetic language, and which is so because it is the true and natural expression of individuality, will be wanting. Even the genius and ardour of Dr. Furnivall must fail to disinter the soft pearl of distinction from the heaped potsherds and broken brickbats of a violent and self-imposed originality of diction, however great the natural and acquired faculties of the poet may be; yes, even though such faculties be far greater than those of others who may have added to their generally inferior abilities the art of "expressing *themselves.*" Self must, however, be eliminated from a man's consciousness before the "how," which is the first essential in art, can make itself heard above the voice of the comparatively insigcant "what." To many persons this setting of the manner before the matter must appear almost immoral. Shall the virtues of eagerness and earnestness in pursuit of one's own true good and that of mankind be put after such a trifle as the mode of professing them? The truth, however, is that such eagerness and earnestness are not virtues but rather proofs that virtue is not yet attained, just as the desire for praise is a proof that praise is not fully deserved. Repose "marks the manners of the great," for it is the expression of a degree of attainment which makes all further attainment that is desired easy, sure, and unexciting, and of a modesty which refuses to regard self as the "hub of the universe," without which it cannot revolve, or indeed as in any way necessary to its existence and well-being, however much it may concern a man's own well-being that he should take his share, to the best of his abilities, in doing the good which will otherwise be done without him. The worst hindrance to distinction in nearly all the poetry of our generation is the warm interest and responsibility which the poets have felt in the improvement of mankind; as if—

"Whether a man serve God or his own whim,
Much matters, in the end to any one but him!"

But, to recur again from Art to Life, the virtuous Democrat is always a little Atlas who goes stumbling along with his eye-balls bursting from his head under his self-assumed burthen. Another obstacle to his distinction is his abhorrence of irrationality of all sorts. He dreams of no beauty or excellence beyond the colossal rationality of a Washington or a Franklin; whereas distinction has its root in the irrational. The more lofty, living, and spiritual the intellect and character become, the more is the need perceived for the sap of life which can only be sucked from the inscrutable and, to the wholly rational mind, repulsive ultimates of nature and instinct. The ideal nation of rational Democrats, so far from exemplifying the glory of distinctions, would find its similitude in a great library consisting entirely of duplicates, digests, and popular epitomes of the works of John Stuart Mill.

I confess, therefore, to a joyful satisfaction in my conviction that a real Democracy, such as ours, in which the voice of every untaught ninny or petty knave is as potential as that of the wisest and most cultivated, is so contrary to nature and order that it is necessarily self-destructive. In America there are already signs of the rise of an aristocracy which promises to be more exclusive, and may, in the end, make itself more predominant than any of the aristocracies of Europe; and our own Democracy, being entirely without bridle, can scarcely fail to come to an early, and probably a violent end. There are, however, uses for all things, and those who love justice enough not to care much should disaster to themselves be involved in its execution will look, not without complacency, on the formal and final ruin of superiorities which have not had sufficient care for their honour and their rights to induce them to make even a sincere parliamentary stand for their maintenance. "Superiorities," when they they have reached this stage of decay, are only fit to nourish the fields of future civilisation, as ancient civilisations, gone to rot, have so richly nourished ours; and when Democracy shall have done its temporary work of reducing them to available "mixen," Democracy, too, will disappear, and—after how many "dark ages" of mere anarchy and war and petty fluctuating tyrannies, who can tell?—there will come another period of ordered life and another harvest of "distinguished" men.

In the meantime "genius" and "distinction" will become more and more identified with loudness; floods of vehement verbiage, without any sincere conviction, or indications of the character capable of arriving at one; inhuman humanitarianism; profanity, the poisoner of the roots of life; tolerance and even open profession and adoption of ideas which Rochester and Little would have been ashamed even remotely to suggest; praise of any view of morals, provided it be an unprecedented one; faith in any foolish doctrine that sufficiently disclaims authority.

That such a writer as Walt Whitman should have attained to be thought a distinguished poet by many persons generally believed to have themselves claims to distinction surely more than justifies my forecast of what is coming. That amazing consummation is already come.

Being well satisfied that the world can get on in this, its destined course, without my help, I should not have broken my customary habit in order to trouble it and myself with the expression of my views of "distinction" and its condition, culture, had it not been for the moral obligation, under which, as I have said, any one may, if he likes, consider himself, to write an *Apologia pro moribus suis*, when these have been publicly attacked. I do not trouble the public often, and have never done so about myself. I take silent and real comfort in the fatalism which teaches me to believe that if, in spite of my best endeavours, I cannot write poetry, it is because poetry is not the thing which is wanted from me, and that, when wanted, it will come from somebody else. But to be stigmatised as a "flunkey" and a "savage," by writers eminent for gentleness and orthodox manners, is a different thing. Flunkeyism and savagery, though, as times go, they should be considered as vices condoned by custom, yet *are* vices; and for this and no other reason have I thought it right to explain the views, feelings, and expressions upon the misconception of which these charges have been founded.

But I have also to complain that there has

been a certain amount of carelessness on the part of my accusers. I do think that when the *Guardian* charges me with the sin of having said nothing in the *Angel in the House* about the "Poor," the writer should have remembered the one famous line I have ever succeeded in writing, namely, that in which Mrs. Vaughan is represented as conveying

"A gift of wine to Widow Neale."

I put it in on purpose to show that my thoughts were *not* wholly occupied with cultivated people, though I knew quite well when I did so that it must evoke from the Olympians—as a candid friend, who has access to the sacred Hill, assures me has been the case—thunders of inextinguishable laughter. Again, I am surprised and grieved that a journal, which so well represents and protects an Establishment in which primitive graces and doctrines have of late been revived in so gratifying a manner, should have accused me of carrying my flunkey notions into a future state, with no other proof alleged than my affirmation of the doctrine of the Intercession of Saints, when I say that sinners, through them, approach Divinity—

"With a reward and grace
Unguess'd by the unwash'd boor who hails Him to his
face."

Was it just to assume that by the "unwash'd boor" I meant only the artisan who had not put aside for the Sunday the materials with which he is accustomed to affix his *Imprimatur* to sound literature?

Again, I must say that the writer in the *Spectator*—whose hand is not easily to be mistaken for any but that of the kindest and most conscientious of editors — should not have denounced me as a person of eminently savage disposition, when he must, I think, have remembered that the very last time I saw him I protested to him how completely my feelings were in unison with the mild amenity of Dr. Newman, adding, by way of confirmation, from a poem of my own—

> "O, that I were so gentle and so sweet,
> So I might deal fair Sion's foolish foes
> Such blows!"

He also neglects, I think, to put a fair interpretation upon what he calls my "hatred" and "scorn" of the People. Sir Thomas Browne, in a time when the People were much less disagreeable than they are become in this the day of their predominance, declared that they constituted the only entity which he could say with truth that he sincerely hated. Now Sir Thomas Browne was, as we know from his own assurance, among the sweetest-tempered and least savage of men— as, indeed, I believe that I myself am. Neither Sir Thomas nor I ever meant the least unkindness or affront to any individual. I have examined my conscience carefully, and I find myself in a state of universal charity. I condemn no one to perdition; I am willing to believe that, were we admitted to the secret recesses of their souls, we might discover some apprehension of the living truth of things in Mr. Gladstone, some conscience in Lord Rosebery of the limits which should be put to party complaisance, some candour in the editor of *Truth;* and I am so far from "hating" these or any, in a wicked sense, that, though I cannot love them with the "love of complacency" —as I believe the schoolmen call it, in distinction to the "love of benevolence"—I love them so much with the latter kind of love that I desire heartily the very best that could happen for them, which would be that, for a moment, they should see themselves as they truly are. I cannot help adding — though I think the *tu quoque* rather vulgar—that, when this really excellent politician and critic said that I confounded the select with the elect, he himself was more or less confounding the elect with the electors.

Finally, had I really been a "flunkey"—I cannot get the sting of that word out of me—had I departed from my Darby and Joan notions to please the dainty with descriptions of abnormal forms of affection; had I sought to conciliate the philosophic by insisting that no son can reasonably regard the chastity of his mother as other than an open question; had I endeavoured to allure laughter by such easy combinations of profanity and *patois* as have won for so many a reputation for being vastly humorous; had I, in compliment to abstainers from what is strong, diluted my modicum of spirit with ten times its bulk of the pure element; had I paid even proper attention to the arbiters of fame, how much "earthlier happy" might I now have been! As it is, whether my thoughts are "pinnacled dim in the intense inane" of the "Unknown Eros," or I proffer, in the *Angel in the House*, "a gift of wine to Widow Neale," the Council of Ten or so are alike unsympathetic; in my declining years I have scarcely a Countess on whom I can rely for a dinner; when I die there will be no discerning Dean to bury me, upon his own responsibility, in Westminster Abbey; and on my obscure tombstone some virtuous and thoughtful democrat may very likely scribble, "Here lies the last of the Savages and Flunkeys,"—notwithstanding all I have now said to prove that I am an unpretentious and sweet-tempered old gentleman, who is harmlessly and respectably preparing for a future state, in which he trusts that there will be neither tomahawk nor "plush."

XIX

A MODERN CLASSIC, WILLIAM BARNES

A CLASSICAL work may be roughly defined as a work of a past generation about which every man of liberal education may be expected to know something. To satisfy this description it is not at all necessary that the work should be of intrinsically classical merit. A speech, a sermon, or a pamphlet, has sometimes attained a classical position by the mere accident of its having been the origin or turning-point of a political or religious movement. Some writers of very ordinary quality refuse to be forgotten because the current of contemporary fashion set so strongly in their favour as to become a fact of literary history. Others have become classics by force of quantity rather than of quality; and the right of these to their position is sometimes better than that of either of the above-named sorts, because quantity is a real element of merit, when the quality is good, though it may not be excellent, as a large mass of aquamarine may be of more real value than a very small emerald. Several writers, the main portion of whose writings is of poor account, have become immortal by one work among many, or by a fragment of some work; some by a single song. Those writers who have left nothing but work of classical quality may almost be counted upon the fingers, a good part of the writings of some of the very greatest authors claiming not to be forgotten only for their author's sake. Without affirming, with Lord Bacon, that the stream of time bears up light and worthless things, and submerges the weightiest—a sentence in which it is difficult to discover the writer's proverbial wisdom—there can be little doubt that it has submerged some things of truly classical pretensions, even since the invention of printing provided an immensely increased security against the literal extinction of a book before there has been time to decide upon its merits. In times past, however, though readers were far fewer in number, they seem to have been so much higher in average quality than the readers of our own day, that scarcely any works of real power escaped a sufficient amount of contemporary recognition to insure them some hearing during that space of time which is ordinarily required for testing a work's fitness for fame. Time has not utterly submerged nearly so much writing of the first quality by its mere lapse as has been dragged to the bottom by too vast a weight of circumjacent worthlessness. Fifty good lines will sometimes float five thousand bad or medium ones, yet they may be sunk by twenty or fifty thousand such. Suckling's will survive a hundred more recent fames upon the strength of his poem, *On a Wedding;* but Drayton, whose minor poems contain passages not less exquisite, is fading in the dark shadow cast by his "greater" works. Another fact worth noting is that time, while it steadily sustains the fame of certain writers, detaches it from their best productions. The comparatively unknown "minor poems" of Spenser, for example are, quantity for quantity, of higher significance than the *Faery Queen*, as Milton well discerned, for he has borrowed little or nothing from the latter, but has abundantly appropriated the beauties of the former, to which he is even indebted for what many readers believe to be some of his own most exquisite and characteristic rhythms, especially those of *Lycidas*.

Again, a fame sufficiently enduring to be justly called such, is sometimes subject to severe fluctuations. Pope and Byron are examples. These writers have had their claims to be ranked as great poets supported and attacked with party violence, one side refusing to recognise them as really poets at all, the other, partly provoked by such injustice, claiming for them the highest peak of Parnassus. This conflict, which is still raging, and will probably do so for a long time, might be greatly pacified by reasonable compromise, founded on the truth above asserted—that the real value of a large aquamarine may be more than that of a small emerald. Except in one famous passage in the *Dunciad*, Pope, much of whose writing is faultless in manner, never rose to perfect greatness of style, to such style as entitles a man to fame, and secures it for him, though he may have written no more than fifty lines at such a pitch. Byron never sustained himself even for twenty verses in such a region. Yet it seems absurd to say that, on the whole, Herrick or George Herbert, for example, have a better title to a classical position than Byron or Pope, though the best writing of the two former is as much more exquisite in quality than that of the two latter, except in the single passage above named, as the beauty of a violet or a peach-blossom is than that of a peony or a dahlia. The light of the smallest fixed star is more intense than that of the most lustrous planet; but in the sky of fame Jupiter and Venus will always make a more conspicuous figure than any two of the Pleiades.

Without venturing upon such confident flights of criticism as those of Mr. Frederic Harrison, who dismisses much of Shakespeare's writing as rubbish, it may be safely said that the inequality of many writers of the highest classical position and genius is one of the most extraordinary of the phenomena of mind. The greatest writers, when the spirit forsakes them, often write not only as badly as but worse than commonly sensible people. Milton's *Speech on the Liberty of unlicensed Printing* contrasts strangely with the truculent, vituperative, and unreasoning mass of his other prose writings. In some half a dozen short poems, Coleridge's fountain of inspiration rises, pure and dazzling, to a height no other poet of the present century has attained, while the rest of his verse is a marsh of comparative dulness. Cowley's cold conglomerate of grit is only rarely fused by the poet's fire, but it was no common fire that could, even occasionally, fuse and be fed by such material; and, as long as there are any readers who do not seek the Muses only for *a*-musement, the question, too hastily asked a hundred years ago, "Who now reads Cowley?" will not be answered as the querist expected it to be.

At this time of day, and with the example of the French "Classics" before us, it need not be urged that sustained finish is not the first claim to classical rank; yet sustained finish, in passages at least, is one of the invariable notes of such claim, for absolute and unlaboured finish is the natural accompaniment of those full floods of poetic passion which come upon all true poets, at least in moments. In such happy flood-tides the best words will take their best order in the best metres without any sensible effort; but in most poets these outpourings are rare indeed, though a conscientious worker will sometimes conceal their rarity by spending so much time and labour upon the comparatively uninspired context of passages inspired that his whole work will be upon the same level of verbal beauty, and the delighted peruser will find nothing to remind him that easy reading's sometimes d——d hard writing. There have been few poets who have worked with such conscientiousness, and the reward of such work is far off, for "the crowd, incapable of perfectness," are more moved to admiration by the alternation and contrast of good with bad than by that of different kinds of excellence. This disqualification for immediate recognition is equally shared by another and still rarer order of poet—he who is the ideal "classic," he in whose every verse poetic feeling breathes in words of unlaboured perfection.

I should hesitate to declare my belief that William Barnes, the "Dorset Poet," belongs to this rare order did I not know that my belief is shared by judges of authority better established than mine, one of whom—a well-known and grave and cautious speaker and writer—went so far as to say in my hearing, "There has been no such art since Horace." This saying, of course, implies no sort of comparison of the poetry of Barnes with that of Horace. It simply means that, in both alike, thoughts and feelings are expressed and incidents related and represented with the most dainty perfection; neither does it imply that Barnes is nearly so great a poet as many another whose average display of art has been incomparably less. Burns, for example, who, like Barnes, is a poet of the first water, but not of the first magnitude, is perhaps better at his best than the Dorset poet, though greatly inferior to him in evenness of quality; and permanent fame is right in her usual practice of judging a poet by his best, even when there is not much of it, and in rarely admitting quantity as a main factor of her calculation. That which is of the greatest value in every true artist is his style, and that may be conveyed almost as effectively in fifty pages as in five hundred.

The absolute pre-eminence of style above all other artistic qualities seems not to have been sufficiently perceived or at least insisted upon by critics, and a few words on that subject are therefore proper in a notice of a writer whose individuality, though it may not be so forcible, is more clearly and delicately pronounced than it is in any other poet of our day. That the proper study of mankind is man expresses a truth which Pope had scarcely tenderness and subtlety enough of intellect to feel in its fulness. Some one has better expressed the same thought in the words, " Every soul is a celestial Venus to every other soul." As the human face, the image of the soul, is incomparably the most beautiful object that can be seen by the eyes, the soul itself is the supreme interest and attraction of the intellectual vision ; and the variety of this interest and attraction is only limited by the number of those who, in action, manners, or art, are endowed with the faculty of expressing themselves and their inherent distinction, which, could it be fully displayed, would be found to be absolutely unique in each person. In that shadow of the soul, the face, some glimpse of this fundamental uniqueness is always apparent, no vice or power of custom being enough altogether to quench it. In manners, though singularity is common enough, it is very rarely the clear and expressive outcome of the individual life. When it is so it constitutes "distinction," as it is well called. In art, in which singularity is also common, this living uniqueness is exceedingly rare indeed, and it is what is, rightly again, called "genius," that is, the manifestation of the inward man himself. It has been said that he alone who has no style has true style. It would be better to say that he who has no manner has the first condition of style. As theologians affirm that all a man can of himself do towards obtaining positive sanctity is a negative avoidance of the hindrances of sin, so style, the sanctity of art, can only appear in the artist whose ways are purged, in the hour at least of effective production, from all mannerism, eccentricities, and selfish obfuscation by the external life. These evils are so strong and the individuality of nearly all men so weak, that there is about as much chance of any particular child turning out to be capable of style in art as there is of his being able to fight the battles of Napoleon or to lead the life of St. Francis. There have been whole nations— of which the American is most notable—which have never attained to the production of a single work of art marked by true style.

Now a man's true character or individuality lies, not in his intellect but in his love, not in what he thinks, but what he is. The "light that lighteth every man" is, in every man, the same in kind, though not in degree; he is essentially differentiated from other men by his love. Old writers bore this in mind when they used the words "spirit" and "genius"; what they called spirit we now call wit or talent. "L'esprit est le Dieu des instans, le génie est le Dieu des ages," says Fr. Lebrun. So far are these from being the same that a man may, like Herrick or Blake, be little better than a blank in intellect, yet be full of the dainty perfume of his peculiar love, whilst a colossus of wit and understanding may be as empty as a tulip of the odour of that sanctity; for a sort of sanctity it really is, always containing as it does some manifest relic of that infantine innocence which nearly all men have trodden under foot, or laughed to death, or otherwise lost touch of, before they were out of their teens. This peculiar faculty, or rather virtue, which alone confers true style upon the poet, is as often as not, nay, more often than not, the grace of those whom even ordinarily clever men look down upon, and justly from their point of view, as "little ones." Little ones they mostly are, but their angels behold the face of their Father, and the words of the least of them is a song of individual love which was never heard before and never will be heard again.

To this primary claim to an abiding place among

such minor classics as Herbert, Suckling, Herrick, Burns, and Blake, William Barnes adds that of a sustained perfection of art with which none of them can compare. His language has the continual slight novelty which Aristotle inculcates as proper to true poetic expression, and something much higher than the *curiosa felicitas*, which has been absurdly rendered "curious felicity," but which means the "careful luck" of him who tries many words, and has the wit to know when memory, or the necessity of metre or rhyme, has supplied him unexpectedly with those which are perhaps even better than he knew how to desire. The words of Barnes are not the carefully made clothes, but the body of his thoughts and feelings. Another still rarer praise of his work is that he never stops in it till he has said all that should be said, and never exceeds that measure by a syllable; and about this art there is not the slightest apparent consciousness either of its abundant fulness or its delicate reticence. He seems, in fact, never to have written except under the sense of a subject that makes its own form, and of feelings which form their own words—that is to say, he is always classic both in form and substance.

Perfect, however, as are the *Poems in the Dorset Dialect*, it would be absurd to call Barnes a poet of the first magnitude or even the second. Every one of the minor classics I have named surpasses him in some point of wit, sweetness, subtlety, or force, as he surpasses them in the lovely innocence which breathes from his songs of nature and natural affection. He has written no one poem that time is likely to stamp as of value at all equivalent, for instance, to *Genevieve* or the *Ode on a Grecian Urn;* and such a lyric as Spenser's *Epithalamion*, compared with the best song of Barnes, is as Hera to a wood-nymph.

Barnes's reputation has the great advantage—since he could bear the delay of fame without discouragement—of not having been forced. Poor, contented, unambitious, without anything remarkable in his person or conversation or romantic in his circumstances, hidden all his lifetime in a sequestered country parsonage, and having no means, direct or indirect, of affecting the personal hopes or fears of his literary contemporaries, they have left him alone in his humble glory, which was to recite to delighted audiences of farmers and ploughmen and their wives and sweethearts a series of lyrics, idylls, and eclogues, which, being the faultless expression of elementary feelings and perceptions, are good for all but those in whom such feelings and perceptions are extinct.

The very best of Barnes's poems are almost as bare of "ornament" and as dependent for effect on their perfection, as a whole, as a tragedy of Æschylus. There is not the slightest touch of "poetry" in the language itself of the rustics who are the *dramatis personæ* of the eclogues, yet poetry has not much to show which is more exquisite in its way than these unconscious and artless confabulations of carters and milkmaids as reflected in the consciousness and arranged by the art of the poet.

I will conclude my statement of the claim of Barnes to be regarded as an English classic by a few words on the likelihood, as it seems to me, of his being one of the last of his sort. Everything in the present state and apparent prospects of civilisation is discouraging to the production of classical work. Boys and girls may lisp in numbers because the numbers come, but no true artist in words can do his arduous though joyful work except in the assured hope of having, sooner or later, an audience; and as time goes on this must seem to him a less and less likely reward and complement of his labour. Barnes's best poems have been before the public for more than forty years; yet what proportion of those who will read this notice have ever held a volume of them in their hands? A hundred or two hundred years ago his general acknowledgment by educated readers would have been immediate. The *Religio Medici* was reprinted eight times in England and translated into most languages of Europe during the lifetime of Sir Thomas Browne, its literary excellence constituting its only attraction, for all "parties" were offended by it. The reading public of England was then less than one-tenth of its present number, making a sale of eight editions thus equivalent to one of eighty editions now. The book having been recognised at the time for what it is, a true classic, has continued to form part of the course of reading expected in cultivated persons. But had it been published in our own day, would it have sold eighty copies? We read of £5, £20, or even £60 in old times having been given by booksellers to persons of wholly untried fame for the copyrights of works which time has nevertheless stamped as great classics. It seems scarcely credible, but there can be no reasonable doubt of it. Is it that the present indifference and even repugnance to new excellence of the highest order is accounted for by our having more of the old than we know what to do with? Scarcely; for a man of forty, without being at all a man of unlimited leisure, may very well have perused all that remains of the world's literature that is above or up to the mark of Sir Thomas Browne or William Barnes. The few shelves which would hold all the true classics extant might receive as many more of the like as there is any chance that the next two or three centuries could produce, without burthening the select and leisurely scholar with a sense of how much he had to read. Is it not rather that the power to appreciate either the matter or form of genuine art in writing is dying out, even among those who by their education ought to be the zealous upholders and guardians of a high and pure standard? Lawlessness, self-assertion, oddity instead of individuality, and inorganic polish where there should be the breathing completeness of art, are no longer the delight only of the "groundlings." They are also the lure of leaders of literary fashion, of those whose approval used to be the almost certain forerunner of fame, and that foretaste of it without which the soul of man of genius sickens within him and refuses to exercise its functions. There appears to be little hope that this is only a transitory declension. It is not a reaction but a decay; and the recuperative force, if there be any in the future, shows no signal of its approach. The peace and joy which are the harvest of a quiet mind, and the conditions—when they are not the inspirations, as they were in Barnes—of true art no longer exist. In America, where it has been well said there is everywhere comfort but no joy, and where popularity, as a clever American lady assured me, lasts a year, and fame ten, we probably have the mirror of our own very near future ; and the decline from this present easy-going state of things to the commencement of a series of dark ages, of which no one shall be able to discern the limit, may perhaps be more rapid than most of us imagine. Unpalatable and unacceptable as the suggestion may be, it cannot be denied by persons who are able and willing to look facts in the face that there are already strong indications of a relapse into a long-protracted period of social and political disorganisation, so complete that there shall be no means of leisure or even living for a learned class nor any audience for what it has to impart. Such recrudescences of civilisation have occurred, and they may occur again, though the prospect may be as incredible to most Europeans at the present moment as it must have been to the lieges of the Eternal City at the height and sudden turning-point of its popular glory and seemingly consolidated order. By Americans the idea would of course be scouted. But American culture and civilisation are identical with those of Europe, only they are in many respects the worse and in very few the better for transplantation. Religion, though widespread, is of a vulgarer and less efficient type than among us ; art is absolutely non-existent ; and the vanity which so loudly claims the paternity of the future is the very worst of prognostics for the fulfilment of that expectation. America is beginning where others have ended, in a widely spread and widely indulged desire for riches and luxury. It is said that the disappearance of some of the finest and most carefully cultivated sorts of fruit trees is owing to the fact that the grafts, from which alone they can be reproduced, will only live and give other grafts during the natural lifetime of the original tree. History seems to indicate that a similar law applies to the grafts of culture and civilisation, and that they cannot long survive the failure of the sap in the old trunk.

XX

THE WEAKER VESSEL

IT is "of faith" that the woman's claim to the honour of man lies in the fact of her being the "weaker vessel." It would be of no use to prove what every Christian man and woman is bound to believe, and what is, indeed, obvious to the senses of any sane man and woman whatever. But a few words of random comment on the text may, by adding to faith knowledge, make man and woman—woman especially—more thankful than before for those conditions which constitute the chief felicity of her life and his, and which it is one of the chief triumphs of progress to render ever more and more manifest. The happiest result of the "higher education" of woman cannot fail to consist in the rendering of her weakness more and more daintily conspicuous. How much sweeter to dry the tears that flow because one cannot accede to some demonstrable fallacy in her theory of variable stars, than to kiss her into conformity as to the dinner-hour or the fitness or unfitness of such-or-such a person to be asked to a picnic! How much more dulcet the *dulcis Amaryllidis ira* when Amaryllis knows Sophocles and Hegel by heart, than when her accomplishments extend only to a moderate proficiency in French and the pianoforte! It is a great consolation to reflect that, among all the bewildering changes to which the world is subject, the character of woman cannot be altered; and that, so long as she abstains from absolute outrages against nature—such as divided skirts, free-thinking, tricycles, and Radicalism—neither Greek, nor conic sections, nor political economy, nor cigarettes, nor athletics can ever really do other than enhance the charm of that sweet unreasonableness which humbles the gods to the dust and compels them to adore the lace below the last hem of her brocade! It is owing to this ineradicable perfection that time cannot change nor custom stale her infinite variety.

A French writer has complained that there are not more than about twenty-five species of woman. Had not his senses been Frenchified, he would have perceived that every woman is a species in herself — nay, many species. The aspects of reason are finite, but those of unreason infinite;

and, so long as one woman is left in the world, no poet can want a perfectly unspoilt subject, and one which can never be fathomed. Some poet has, with much *vraisemblance*, represented Jove as creating woman in order that there might be at least one thing in the universe that should have for him the zest of unintelligibility—which nothing but weakness and unreason could supply. The human creature, however, is incapable of the absolutely incomprehensible; therefore it has been providentially devised that no man should be without some touch of womanhood, and no woman without some manhood. Were it otherwise, they would be wholly uninteresting to one another, and could no more mix than oil and water. This reciprocal tincture of each other's sex produces that mixture of inscrutability and comprehensibility in the well-constituted and well-matched man and woman, and that endless misunderstanding, mitigated by obscure insight, which, if not the original cause of love, is the source of that perpetual agitation of the feelings which indefinitely increases love, and without which love, if it did not die, would at least go to sleep. "Fax agitando magis ardescit."

Most of the failures in marriage come of the man's not having manhood enough to assert the prerogatives which it is the woman's more or less secret delight to acknowledge. She knows her place, but does not know how to keep it unless he knows it also; and many an otherwise amiable woman grows restless and irritable under the insupportable doubt as to whether she has got her master. In order to put the question to the test, she does things she knows he is bound to resist or resent, in the hope of being put down with a high hand, and perhaps a bad word or two—since even the mildest corporal chastisement has gone out with the heroic days of such lovers as Siegfried and Kriemhild.

Friendship and love differ mainly in this: that, whereas the felicity of friendship consists in a mutual interchange of benefits, intellectual and otherwise, that of love is in giving on one part and receiving on the other, with a reciprocal perception of how sweet it is to the endower to endow and the receiver to receive. This relation involves, as ancient philosophers and theologians have observed, a certain opulence on the one side and a corresponding destitution on the other—a destitution which, however, is the greatest opulence in the eyes of the former as being the necessary condition of his proper delight, which is to endow. The myth of King Cophetua and the Beggar-Maid is representative of the most perfect nuptial relationship.

All joy worth the name is in equal love between unequals; and the inmost delight of giving honour lies in its being of voluntary favour, and of receiving it in the perception that the rendering of it is an infatuation of love on the part of the giver. Desert cares as little for honour as it is in the habit of receiving it. The vanity of a woman need not derogate from that sense of comparative nothingness which is to herself the sweetest part of the offering of her affection. Indeed, her vanity may be based upon this sense of her smallness; as knowing that this is the source of her attractiveness. A woman without the vanity which delights in her power of attracting would be by that very fact without power to attract; for she would want the power to receive that which the man delights to give—namely, that tender corroboration and consummation of her sense of her own sweetness, which every lover imagines that he of all men is alone able to confer upon her.

As to the unreason of woman, there is a positive character about it which elevates it from defect into a sort of sacred mystery. "Perhaps," says Thomas Hardy, the greatest living authority on the subject, "in no minor point does woman astonish her helpmate more than in the strange power she possesses of believing cajoleries that she knows to be false, except, indeed, in that of being utterly sceptical on strictures which she knows to be true." Philip van Artevelde says— with perfect truth as to the fact, but with a most erroneous implied inference—"How little flattering is a woman's love!" They understand little of love who do not see how great a part is played in it by mirth and paradox, and how the surprise of finding oneself loved the more for a kiss or a compliment makes up abundantly for the disappointment of discovering that the greatest merits or self-sacrifice do not count for much in comparison.

When the Father of Gods and men presented the newly created woman to the Council of Olympus, we know that she was greeted with peals of laughter; and to this day there is nothing that a woman of well-balanced mind hates more in a man than his taking her too much *au grand sérieux.*

It has been the practice of the Catholic Church not to define a dogma, or to promulgate it as a necessary part of faith, until it has come to be widely denied; and that Church to which all truly sensible persons, be they Catholic or otherwise, belong, is ever careful to abstain from formulating doctrines so long as they continue to constitute portions of the implicit and active belief of mankind in general. Words tend to obscure and blunt the edge of truth, which is better felt than spoken; but when it is no longer generally felt, and is widely spoken against, then there is no help for it but to hurl anathemas against its deniers. Now it is high time that it should be plainly declared that there are few more damnable heresies than the doctrine of the equality of man and woman. It strikes at the root of the material and spiritual prosperity and felicity of both, and vitiates the whole life of society in its source. From time to time in the world's past history, the inferiority and consequent subordination of woman have been denied by some fanatic or insignificant sect of fanatics, and the cudgels have been taken up for man by some busybody in his premature dread of the "monstrous regiment of women"; but the consensus of the world has until lately been dead against the notion. Every man Jack would have listened with a cheery laugh at the setting up of a claim of equality on the part of his dame Jill; and Aristotle, Bacon, and St. Thomas Aquinas would have regarded with silent wonder the idea of raising to an equal rank with her lord the *placens uxor* whom the Angelical Doctor declares to be "scarcely a reasonable creature." Here and there, indeed, a "poet sage" has glorified the woman in terms that, taken literally, are violently heterodox; but everybody knew what he meant in thus making a divinity of her whose very excellence consists in her being decidedly a little lower than the angels—those transmitters of the divinity of which she is only the last reflector. Lovers, also, have in all ages practised a playful idolatry; and if they are beginning now to drop the language of hyperbole, it is because they are liable now to be believed. The ideal position of woman towards man, according to the doctrine of the Church—which, in this instance at least, is verifiable by all who have the power of psychological observation—is that of his reflection or "glory." She is the sensible glory or praise of his spiritual wisdom, as the rising cloud of incense is that of the invisible sunshine, which, passing through the painted window, becomes manifest in all its rainbow hues only when it strikes upon the otherwise colourless vapour. The world—which sometimes fancies that it is being extremely cynical when it is only expressing emphatically some Christian and philosophical verity—expresses this fact when it says that the virtue of woman is the noblest invention of man. She has not the strength for, or indeed the knowledge of, true virtue and grace of character, unless she is helped to that knowledge and strength by the man.

"He for God only, she for God in him."

She only really loves and desires to become what

he loves and desires her to be; and beauty, being visible or reflected goodness, can only exist in woman when and in proportion as the man is strong, good, and wise. When man becomes womanish, and ceases to be the transmitter of the heavenly light of wisdom, she is all abroad, she does not know what to do with herself, and begins to chatter or scream about her rights; but, in this state, she has seldom understanding enough to discern that her true right is to be well governed by right reason, and, instead of pouring contempt on her degraded companion for his spiritual impotence, she tries all sorts of hopeless tricks—the most hopeless of all being that of endeavouring to become manly—in order the better to attract him who has become womanish.

To maintain that man and woman are equals in intelligent action is just as absurd as it would be to maintain that the hand that throws a ball and the wall that casts it back are equal. The woman has an exquisite perception and power of admiring all the man can be or do. She is the "glory" of his prowess and nobility in war, statesmanship, arts, invention, and manners; and she is able to fulfil this, her necessary and delightful function, just because she is herself nothing in battle, policy, poetry, discovery, or original intellectual or moral force of any kind.

The true happiness and dignity of woman are to be sought, not in her exaltation to the level of man, but in a full appreciation of her inferiority and in the voluntary honour which every manly nature instinctively pays to the weaker vessel. In the infinite distance between God and man, theologians find the secret of the infinite felicity of divine love; and the incomparable happiness of love between the sexes is similarly founded upon their inequality. The playfulness which is the very dainty and "bouquet" of love, comes of the fact that in the mutual worship of lovers there is always a tacit understanding of something of a King Cophetua and Beggar-Maid relationship. No right-minded woman would care a straw for her lover's adoration if she did not know that he knew that after all he was the true divinity.

There is a mystic craving in the great to become the love-captive of the small, while the small has a corresponding thirst for the enthralment of the great.

> " 'Tis but in such captivity
> The boundless heavens know what they be."

The central prophecy in the Old Testament is that "A man shall be compassed by a woman."

This wonder, which is applied by the Prophet to higher things, is also the secret of human love and its marvellous order. The infinite circumscribed by the finite, the great by the small, is the insoluble paradox which teases human affection with inexhaustible delight, as it is the thought which kindles and keeps alive the devotion of the Saint.

When this order ceases to exist, and with it the life and delight of love, it is wholly the man's fault. A woman will only consent to be small when the man is great; but then she sets no bounds to her sweet self-humiliation, and by becoming the slave of his reason she reduces him to a like captivity to her desires. The widely extended impatience of women under the present condition of things is nothing but an unconscious protest against the diminished manliness of men. When a large proportion of our male population are thrilled with effeminate pain if an injury is done to the skin of a cat or of an Irish rebel, but feel no indignation or anguish at the violation of every sound principle and the deadening of every sentiment that ennobles life, women feel that the external conditions of true womanhood have disappeared; and it is not to be wondered at if many of them, unclothed, as it were, of the sentiment of surrounding manhood, should, in their ignorant discomfort and despair, make as unsightly a spectacle of themselves as does the animal called a hermit-crab when, by some chance, it is ejected, bare, comfortless, and unprotected, from the shell of its adoption.

XXI

MADAME DE HAUTEFORT

THERE is nothing comparable for moral force to the charm of truly noble manners. The mind is, in comparison, only slightly and transiently impressed by heroic actions, for these are felt to be but uncertain signs of a heroic soul; nothing less than a series of them, more sustained and varied than circumstances are ever found to demand, could assure us, with the infallible certainty required for the highest power of example, that they were the faithful reflex of the ordinary spirit of the actor. The spectacle of patient suffering, though not so striking, is more morally impressive; for we know that

> "Action is transitory—a step, a blow,
> The motion of a muscle this way or that—
> 'Tis done; and, in the after vacancy,
> We wonder at ourselves like men betray'd;
> Suffering is permanent, obscure, and dark,
> And has the nature of infinity."

The mind, however, has a very natural repugnance to the sustained contemplation of this species of example, and is much more willingly persuaded by a spectacle precisely the reverse—namely, that of goodness actually upon the earth triumphant, and bearing in its ordinary demeanour, under whatever circumstances, the lovely stamp of obedience to that highest and most rarely-fulfilled commandment, "Rejoice evermore." Unlike action or suffering, such obedience is not so much the way to heaven, as a picture, say rather a part, of heaven itself; and truly beautiful manners will be found upon inspection to involve a continual and visible compliance with that apostolical injunction. A right obedience of this kind must be the crown and completion of all lower kinds of obedience. It is not compatible with the bitter humiliations of the habit of any actual sin; it excludes selfishness, since the condition of joy, as distinguished from pleasure, is generosity, and a soul in the practice of going forth from itself; it is no sensual partiality for the "bright side" of things, no unholy repugnance to the consideration of sorrow; but a habit of lifting life to a height at which all sides of it become bright, and all moral difficulties intelligible: in action it is a salubrity about which doctors will not disagree; in the countenance it is a loveliness about which connoisseurs will not dispute; in the demeanour it is a lofty gentleness, which, without pride, patronises all the world, and which, without omitting the minutest temporal obligations or amenities, does everything with an air of immortality. When Providence sets its inheritors upon a hill where they cannot be hid, acknowledging, as it were, their deserts by conferring upon them conspicuous fortune and corporeal advantages, and proving them by various and splendid opportunities, the result is an example to which, as we have said, there is nothing else to be compared in the way of moral agency; a spectacle so clear in the demonstration of human majesty and loveliness, that the honouring of it with love and imitation is the only point of worship upon which persons of all countries, faiths, customs, and morals, are in perfectly catholic agreement. For the benefit of a single such example it were scarcely possible that the world could pay too dearly. Monarchy and aristocracy have nothing to fear from the arguments of their opponents so long as democracies have failed to produce a Sidney or a Bayard, a Lady Rachel Russell or a Madame de Hautefort.

It is far from our intention to imply that the loveliest blossoms of humanity appear, like the flowers of the aloe, at centenary intervals, and then only in king's gardens. We are not allowed to doubt but that the poor and suffering most often are what "the rich should be, right-minded"; and that they therefore, more frequently than the rich, have the foundation of right manners. Nevertheless, spiritual loveliness when found in conspicuous places, and "clothed upon" with extraordinary personal and intellectual gifts, while it is more impressive than humble worth in the sight even of the best, as being exposed to subtler temptations to deny itself, is made visible to many who would refuse to acknowledge the same lustre were it shining in a dark place, and is more imposing to all, not only because all are naturally delighted with the extraordinary occurrence of harmony between the apparently hostile realms of grace and nature, fortune, and desert, but also because such harmony explains, exalts, and really completes its seemingly-opposed elements, and grace, expressing itself with thorough culture and knowledge of the world, becomes natural, and nature, instructed in its true perfection, gracious. Moreover, fine manners are always more or less an art, and this art is one which the poor and socially obscure have no means of bringing to perfection: their lives may be purified in the furnace of affliction, and worked by the blows of circumstance into the finest temper; faith and resignation may give evenness, and love a certain lustre to their demeanour; but the last touch, which is that which polishes the mirror, and tells more in the eyes of the world than all the rest, is the work of art. And, let it be acknowledged, none of the fine arts is so fine as that of manners, and, of all, it is probably the only one which is cultivated in the next world as well as in this, where also it is, like its sisters, immortal; for the contagion of fine manners is irresistible, and wherever the possessor of them moves, he leaves behind him lovers and imitators who indefinitely, if not infinitely, propagate his likeness. Unlike the lower arts of poetry, music, architecture, and painting, which may be regarded as secondary and derivative from this primary art of good manners, which imitates nothing but God; unlike these arts, in which men have always been the most excellent professors, that of fine manners has been carried to its highest perfection by women. Than some of these, in whom station, beauty, wit, and holiness, have been united, it seems scarcely possible that the angels themselves should shine with a more bright and amiable lustre.

Women, not to speak of their beauty, their docile and self-adaptive natures, and that inherent aptitude for goodness which makes devotion their chief intemperance, enjoy, in their privilege of subordination to men, a vast advantage for the development of the noblest manners. Obedience is the proper perfection of humanity; fine manners are the expression of that perfection; and that obedience and consequent perfection are likely to be frequent and complete in proportion as the object to which submission is directly due is near and comprehensible. Remote and incomprehensible Deity is the "head of the man"; and his obedience to that vast and invisible authority, though of a loftier nature, is necessarily incomplete in its character and indistinct in its expression, when compared with the submission of the woman to the image of the same authority in himself. While the one obeys from faith, the other does so from sight; and the sensible "*beauty* of holiness" is therefore almost exclusively the prerogative of the woman. The light of her duty strikes directly upon that to which it is relative, and is reflected back in loveliness upon herself; while his appears to be lost in the space it has to traverse to its object. Here is a great spiritual distinction of sex, which those who reject the doctrine of subordination confound and destroy; pulling down the majesty of man by abolishing his principal responsibility, and turning the peculiar strength and glory of the woman into weakness and disgrace.

There was one place and time singular in the history of the world for the development of the woman's character to the extreme limit of her capacities in various directions. The court of France in the reign of Louis XIII., the regency of Anne of Austria, and the early part of the reign of Louis XIV., produced a company of ladies, in whose presence all the remaining tract of history looks dim. The wars of the League had left the great nobles of France in the enjoyment of an amount of personal freedom, importance, and dignity, greater than was ever, before or since, the lot of any aristocracy. Chivalrous traditions; the custom of appeal to arms for the settlement of personal quarrels, a custom which is said to have cost the country some nine hundred of its best gentlemen in about nine years; the worship of womanhood carried to a pharisaical strictness of observance, were conditions which, though socially disastrous in various ways, exalted the individual *valeur* of men to the most imposing height, and rendered a corresponding exaltation imperative upon the women, in order to secure that personal predominance which it is their instinct to seek. The political state of France was one which afforded the members of its court extraordinary occasions for the display of character. That state was one of a vast transition. Feudal privileges had to be either moderated, defined, and constitutionalised, or else destroyed. The revolution which was about to operate in England and to end in liberty, was working in France with a manifestly opposite destiny. Richelieu and Mazarin were slowly and surely bringing about an absolute despotism, as the only solution of the political difficulties of the state consistent with its greatness, and, probably, even with its unity. The opposition of the nobles to the diminution of their power was carried on with far greater boldness and grandeur of personal effect, inasmuch as it was done without directly affronting the monarchical authority in the persons of its weak representations, Louis XIII. and Anne of Austria. The two great ministers were the objects against which the whole wrath of the nobility was directed. Hence the war against encroaching monarchy was in great part waged in the court itself; and the king and the queen-regent were themselves found from time to time in the ranks of the indignant aristocracy. Here, then, was a wonderful field for individual effect; and that field was open to women no less, or even more, than to men; for the struggle, indeed, on the part of the latter was, upon the whole, a selfish and ignoble one; no national idea inspired it; every one was for himself and his house; and the women were perfectly able to sympathise and assist in quarrels of this personal and intelligible interest. Richelieu and Mazarin were moreover exactly the kind of enemies to excite the peculiar hostility, and prove the peculiar talents of women. In their modes of thought and action, these ministers were too much like women not to be naturally obnoxious to their hatred. In these days, too, rose Port-Royal, with its female reformers, saints, and theologians, offering an asylum to weary and repentant worldliness and passion, or a fresh field for vanity which had exhausted its ordinary irritants. On every side lay great temptations and great opportunities; and the women of the period seem to have been endowed with singular qualifications for the illustration of both. Of this constellation of splendid personalities, Marie de Hautefort was the crowning glory.

She was born in 1616, and was soon after left an orphan and committed to the charge of her grandmother, Madame de la Flotte Hauterive. Her early years were passed in the country; but there was much talk of the court and its pleasures at her grandmother's house; and the beautiful and intellectual girl, at eleven years of age—then almost a woman in figure—and then and always too innocent to have any element of asceticism in her sincere piety, offered fervent prayers to Heaven to be allowed to—*go to court!* Madame de la Flotte had affairs which brought her to Paris; Marie went with her, and made such an impression, that the queen-mother, Mary de Medicis, at once placed her among her maids-of-honour. Though but twelve years of age, her manners were distinguished by that "très grand air, tempéré par une retenue presque sévère," which to the last continued to be the quality of her chaste and noble loveliness. Her beauty of person must have been of the very loftiest kind, if we may judge from the effect which she immediately produced in the most brilliant and fastidious court in the world. She had the name of Aurora given to her, as descriptive of her fresh and innocent splendour. When she was fourteen the king fell in love with her. He took her away from the queen-mother, and placed her with the queen-consort, who at first was naturally somewhat shy of a maid-of-honour who was manifestly a rival. But Anne soon discovered in Mademoiselle de Hautefort a mind from which she had nothing to dread. As for the *affections* of the king, Anne enjoyed too little of them at any time to care much for the platonic alliance which she saw plainly was the worst she had to fear; she soon found also that her misfortunes and neglect constituted a much more powerful claim to the noble girl's attachment than the power and prestige of the greatest monarch in the world. Thus the favourite of the king enjoyed the singular distinction of being at the same time scarcely less the favourite of his wife. The first public mark of attention from the king to the maid-of-honour was on occasion of a sermon, at which the queen and the court were present. The maids-of-honour, according to custom, were seated on the ground. The king sent the velvet, on which he was kneeling, for Mademoiselle de Hautefort to sit upon. She blushed with confusion, obeyed a sign from the queen to take it, but placed it by her side. Such a mixture of modesty and tact was not unappreciated in the court of France. On another occasion an incident occurred which will serve to explain how the position of Mademoiselle de Hautefort was one against which not the slightest exception could be taken, a little allowance being made for the liberal manners of the seventeenth century. The king entered the apartment of the queen as she and her maid-of-honour were discussing a note, containing something that it was not desired that the king should see. He pressed very much to obtain it, and Mademoiselle de Hautefort found it impossible to keep the queen's secret except by placing the paper in her bosom. This at once terminated the dispute; although the queen in jest held the hands of the beautiful girl, and dared the king to take the letter from its sanctuary. Though the religion of Louis, and his reverence for this noble lady, prevented him from affronting her with his passion, his extreme jealousy was a source of continual annoyance to her; and many a time the pride of the good and gay young beauty resented the assiduities and pretensions of an *amitié* which had no right to such exclusiveness, and no foundations for such suspicions; for, with several of the noblest gentlemen of France at her feet, Mademoiselle de Hautefort's heart was untouched. After these misunderstandings with his "friend," Louis would sit and sulk in a corner for hours; and there was no gaiety at the court until a good understanding was restored. At this time the affections of the maid-of-honour were chiefly set upon her mistress, for whose sake alone she seems to have endured attentions which, to say the least, incommoded her. Madame de Motteville, in her Memoirs, assures us that Mademoiselle de Hautefort treated Louis at all times "as badly as it was permitted to treat a king." His neglect and hatred of his wife, founded upon the atrocious suspicions which Richelieu, for political purposes, succeeded in bringing upon her, deprived him of the respect of one whose generous nature revolted against all appearance of injustice. Towards Richelieu himself, as the chief author of the queen's misfortunes, she entertained feelings of contempt and dislike which she made no effort to conceal, although the mighty minister loaded her with compliments and attentions, calculating that her presence at the court was not fitted to increase the favour of Anne with Louis. Finding, however, that all his endeavours to change her from an enemy into a friend were vain, and that she was doing more service to the queen by pleading her cause than disservice by her personal attractions, Richelieu determined upon getting rid of her influence. He persuaded the king that she ridiculed his manners and his passion in his absence; and, instead of appeasing his scruples of conscience, as heretofore, he represented his affection as dangerous and contrary to religion. These means proving only partially effective, Richelieu called into play a rival beauty, Louise Angélique de la Fayette, who, with scarcely inferior virtues and personal attractions, had a nature more sympathetic with that of Louis. The king found in this lady a compassionate, patient, and friendly listener to the sorrows and complaints which he delighted in talking about to women; and their relationship soon ripened into the high and tender friendship which was ordinarily the limit of the king's "amours"; for, with all his weaknesses, his religion was sincere and his refinement remarkable; and the woman whom he could have suspected of a willingness to sacrifice her dignity to his affection would never have possessed it. In this instance, however, the king in a moment of passion forgot his better knowledge and Mademoiselle de la Fayette's honour so far as to propose that she should take up her residence at Versailles, and be "toute à lui." His punishment was heavy, but just. The noble young lady, between whom and himself there had for two years subsisted a most deep and happy friendship, determined, after many regrets and a strong struggle with her heart, to have no further communication with him but through the grating of a nunnery. Upon these terms, however, the king continued for many months to see her at the convent of St. Mary of the Visitation. Like Mademoiselle de Hautefort, Mademoiselle de la Fayette was constant in her favourable representations of the queen to her consort; and it was after one of these singular visits, that the king, prevented by a storm from returning to St. Maur, stopped a night at the Louvre, where was the queen, who nine months after gave birth to Louis XIV. During this period, Mademoiselle de

Hautefort remained in the service of Anne, who was almost entirely abandoned by Louis, and solaced herself with maintaining, chiefly by means of Madame de Chevreuse, a correspondence with her royal relatives of Spain, then at war with France. The fact of this correspondence was treasonous; and the nature of it, whatever it may have been, was such that the queen had the greatest terror of its transpiring. At one moment her fate depended upon the correspondence of her replies to the examination imposed upon her by Richelieu with the statements of her confidant and aid La Porte, who was then in the Bastille. Mademoiselle de Hautefort, as heroic as she was beautiful and tender, disguised herself *en grisette*, left the Louvre at dawn, went in a *fiacre* alone to the Bastille, waited ever so long exposed to the coarse pleasantries of the *corps de garde* at the gate, obtained a solitary interview with the Chevalier de Jars, who had just received his pardon on the very scaffold for his part in the queen's affairs, prevailed upon him to risk his head again by making himself the means of conveying a letter to La Porte, returned as she came, had the good fortune to reach her apartment unrecognised; and was then for the first time overcome with the terrible risks to which she had exposed herself, and, what she prized far more, her unblemished reputation. In the political intrigues of the queen and Madame de Chevreuse she had no interest. Richelieu and the king were unjust; Anne suffered, and required service and consolation; and that was all the noble maiden knew or cared to know.

The prospect of the queen's becoming a mother, as soon as it was known, made a great improvement in her position with the king, who was thus again thrown into the society of Mademoiselle de Hautefort. His passion, for a time suspended by his affection for Mademoiselle de la Fayette, revived, and maintained for two years more its chaste and stormy life. The proud maiden refused to acquire any advantage to her not very splendid fortune; and the only honour she consented to receive was one from the hands of the queen—namely, the office of *dame d'atours*, which entitled her to be called Madame. Richelieu's jealousies reawakened with the passion of the king; there was no second Louise de la Fayette at hand; and the minister took advantage of the part which he had the means of proving that Mademoiselle de Hautefort had taken in aiding the queen in her forbidden correspondence with Madame de Chevreuse and other active enemies of the cardinal, to demand the dismissal of the favourite from the court. Louis resisted. Richelieu had recourse to his last and always successful trick: he gave the king to understand that he must choose between his minister and his mistress. Even this argument, however, only prevailed upon Louis to consent to her being exiled for a period of fourteen days. She refused to believe the direction to absent herself, on receiving it through Richelieu, and obtained an audience of the king, demanding of what crime she was accused. Louis replied that the order was wrung from him against his will; that it was but for temporary reasons of state, and that it gave him the greatest grief. This was not enough to satisfy the dignity and self-respect of the lady, who told him that in bidding him adieu for fourteen days she bade him adieu for ever. Mademoiselle de Chémerault, another of the queen's ladies, was dismissed at the same time; but only in order that she might continue to act as Richelieu's spy upon the words and actions of the noble creature, who fancied her her sincere friend. Mademoiselle de Hautefort thought that the queen had not treated Mademoiselle de Chémerault with sufficient generosity in the gifts she made her on her dismissal; and, utterly careless of her own interests, she addressed to Anne the noblest letter of remonstrance which it has ever been our happiness to read. Louis died without beholding her again;

and, indeed, his fickle nature had been diverted from his sorrow for her loss by a new favourite, Cinq Mars. Anne was no sooner a widow than she begged Madame de Hautefort to return. She was now twenty-seven, and at the height of her beauty. She became the chief ornament of the famous Maison Rambouillet—at that time the place of reunion for the most refined and exclusive society the world has seen. Here, surrounded by the atmosphere of literary dilettantism, which turned all her contemporaries more or less into blue-stockings, and which in its less dignified development at the assemblies of Mademoiselle de Scudéry afterwards provoked the ridicule of Molière, Madame de Hautefort's delicacy and tact preserved her from the airs of the *précieuse*. The few letters of her writing which remain are "toujours spirituelles, mais très négligées"; and a contemporary writer says, "Pour les vers, c'est sa passion : et, quoiqu'elle n'en fasse point, *elle les récite comme si elle les faisait.*" As she was free from the prevailing intellectual dilettantism, she was equally a stranger to the more tempting, and, at that time, all but universal dilettantism of the affections. The consequence was, that the passions she inspired were deep, sincere, and really chivalrous. The mock chivalry of La Rochefoucauld became genuine towards her. On the eve of a battle he gave her brother a letter, containing a declaration of his love, to be given to her if he died; if not, to be returned. "C'était là," says M. Cousin, "comme on faisait la cour à Mlle. de Hautefort." Her nobler charms for a while eclipsed the attractions of Madame de Chevreuse in the eyes of Charles of Lorraine. On one occasion he took prisoner a French gentleman whom he discovered to be slightly acquainted with her. "I give you your liberty," he said; "and require nothing for your ransom but the honour of hearing that you have kissed, upon my part, the hem of the robe of Madame de Hautefort." And many another, in whom love had hitherto been vice, found it the well-head of virtue when inspired by her. A noble young soldier, the Marquis de Gêvres, had the inexpressible honour and happiness of touching the heart of this lady; but her royal admirer prevented their marriage, which was in course of arrangement; and, just as De Gêvres was restored to his hopes by the king's death, and was about to receive the staff of Marshal of France for his brilliant services, he was killed at the siege of Thionville. Madame de Hautefort's magnificent reserve upon all points touching her *own* interests and feelings permitted to none of the aristocratic memoir-writers of the time the means of informing posterity how far she was affected by these incidents.

Madame de Hautefort, on her return to the court of Anne of Austria, after the death of Richelieu and Louis XIII., had every reason to calculate upon reaping the reward of her faithful services, as far as such services can be rewarded temporally, in the unimpeded favour of the queen, who was now a queen indeed. But this change from the position of the powerless and oppressed consort to the absolute regent was not really favourable to Madame de Hautefort. She cared very little for politics, and very much for her personal friends; and she was not prepared to look coldly upon all her old alliances, formed at first in the service and interest of the queen, merely because Anne, with a sense of responsibility which made the sacrifice a virtue in *her*, chose to abandon her former connections, and to take up with the partisans of Richelieu and the monarchy. The loyalty of Madame de Hautefort was of too high and heavenly a character for that. Her position at court, which she by no means undervalued, might still, however, have been maintained, had it not been for the peculiar favour to which Mazarin now rose, and the scandal created by his nightly conferences with the queen. It was more than the pride and delicacy of the *dame d'atours* could bear. Moreover, she was *dévote* full twenty years before the usual age,—for she was now only twenty-seven, and in all the splendour of her beauty; and affairs of state, which were made the excuse for these conferences, were trifles in her eyes when compared with a wilful indifference to even the "appearance of evil." She regarded silence under these circumstances as a crime; and, far from being intimidated by the dangers of interference and expostulation, those dangers acted as provocatives to a virtue of which the only drawback was a heroic intemperance, and a slight defect of suavity when, but only when, it had to do with the failings of kings and queens. In fact, Madame de Hautefort treated Anne, in her turn, "as ill as it was permitted to treat a queen"; that is to say, she displayed a marked disapproval of her conduct, and made no concealment of her dislike of Mazarin, which was unmitigated, although he, like Richelieu, did his very best to be well with her. Failing, he, like his predecessor, determined to get rid of her uncongenial influence; and the very means which Richelieu had used with Louis XIII., Mazarin employed with his royal mistress. He represented Madame de Hautefort as being in the habit of *publicly* expressing her views of the queen's conduct; and Anne, already irritated by the private representations of her *dame d'atours*, was completely estranged from her in heart by the calumnies and exaggerations of the minister. But to dismiss her from the court was not a step to be taken in haste. Madame de Hautefort was the idol of two very considerable parties, the Importants and the Saints; and in the court itself she was without an enemy beside Mazarin, and the mistress whom she persisted in serving too well. The little king, Louis XIV., was devotedly attached to her, and used to call her his wife; and several of the chief nobles of the country were suitors for her hand; in particular, Gassion, the general-in-chief of the French cavalry, the Duke de Liancour, and the Duke Charles de Schomberg, who were among the most valuable servants of the monarchy, were devoted to this lady with a passion which would not have forgiven any injury to her. The Duke de Schomberg seemed to be favoured by Madame de Hautefort; and it was highly to Mazarin's interest that an alliance should take place which would make her the wife of a man who hated partisanship, and would at least secure her neutrality towards the chief minister whom he served. The duke is thus painted by a contemporary: " Il avait les premières charges de la cour; il ne voyait que les princes au-dessus de lui. Il était fait à peu près comme on dépeint les héros de romans:

il était noir ; mais sa mine haute, guerrière, et majestueuse, inspirait du respect à ses amis et de la crainte à ses ennemis ; il était magnifique, libéral, et avait fait des dépenses extraordinaires dans les emplois qu'il avait eu en commandant les armées de France. Sa mine était tellement pleine de majesté, qu'un jour, étant chez une dame et étant dans la ruelle avec un habit fort brillant d'or et d'argent, une nourrice de cette dame entrant dans la chambre en fut si surprise qu'elle s'approcha d'une demoiselle et lui demanda quel roi était là auprès de sa maîtresse ?" A man, in externals at least, not unworthy of our heroine. But her true and stately soul did nothing in haste. She subjected her suitor's passion to the test of a long and dubious courtship; and felt herself bound not to abandon the court, as she probably might have to do for Languedoc, which was his government, until all had been done to retrieve the queen from her position with Mazarin; who was thus at length compelled to obtain by open rupture what he had hoped to effect quietly, and as if in the interest of his proud and beautiful enemy. The party of the Importants were scattered by a sort of *coup d'état;* several even of the ladies about the queen's person were dismissed or warned; and Madame de Hautefort, of all Mazarin's political enemies, was the only one of any consequence who escaped defeat and humiliation on this occasion. *She* was far above suspicion of having had any part in the conspiracy which threw so many others into Mazarin's power; the candour and openness of her enmity puzzled and awed the prince of intriguers, and enabled her to dispute his influence with the queen, long after all the Importants, including the infinitely clever Madame de Chevreuse, were for the time put to silence. Madame de Hautefort was, moreover, to the party of the Saints what Madame de Chevreuse was to the Importants; and her opposition to Mazarin was made formidable by being supported with the whole influence of the *religieuses* of the convents of the Filles-de-Sainte-Marie, the Carmelites, and the Val-de-Grâce. But the warfare thus carried on afforded no cause for open accusation; and it was upon the always somewhat rash generosity of Madame de Hautefort in interceding for those whom she considered to have been unjustly treated, that her fall from court favour was made to depend. She irritated the queen greatly by representations in favour of Beaufort, in whose guilt she did not believe; and on one occasion was so emphatic in recommending the claims of some old servant to Anne's consideration, that the queen told her plainly that she was weary of her reprimands, and altogether dissatisfied with her conduct; and the next morning the *dame d'atours* received a command to quit the court. For a time she was in despair at having, as it appeared, irrevocably offended her to whose service her entire life had been devoted. Like Louise Angélique de la Fayette, she withdrew to the convent of Filles-de-Sainte-Marie, with the intention of becoming one of the *religieuses;* but, happily for the world, her lovely light was destined not to be so hidden under a bushel. Her adorers showed the sincerity of their vows by hastening to renew them now that she was in disgrace. The Duke de Schomberg's solicitations were listened to; and Madame de Hautefort, after a crowning act of nobility which we have not space to relate, but which involved a momentary giving up of her lover for the supposed interests of his family, became the Duchess de Schomberg at the age of thirty, in the year 1646. For ten years she was the tenderest and happiest of wives, and afterwards the holiest of widows. Her personal beauty increased with years, as perfectly noble beauty always does. As she had been the ornament of the Maison Rambouillet without affectation of literature, she now became that of Port-Royal without mixing herself with the Jansenist quarrel. It was in vain that Louis XIV. endeavoured to persuade her back to the court, "afin," as he said, "d'y rétablir la dignité et la grandeur qu'on commence à ne plus y voir." She led a life of active and unpretentious piety until 1691, which was the date of her translation from a life of grace to one of glory.

Where else shall we find another like her? Lady Rachel Russell, her contemporary, was nearer to her than any other we remember; an additional example in confirmation of the remark that nature is fond of bringing forth extraordinary persons in pairs; but Lady Russell seems neither to have had that magnificent physique, nor those splendid opportunities, which confer such a grand and full perfection on the picture of Madame de Hautefort. Do what we will with our understandings and moral principles, we can never make puritans of our tastes; and however the mind may cry *peccavi* for its preference, of two beautiful natures it always will prefer that which goes the most gloriously clad. Neither will the feelings accept potentialities for actualities. Lady Russell, in Madame de Hautefort's circumstances, almost certainly would have been no less noble; nay, it is more than likely that she would have avoided Madame de Hautefort's one mistake, which seems to have been an unnecessarily plain-spoken way towards those who happened to have the power of resenting it with overwhelming effect. As it was, however, Lady Russell's opportunities were limited; and so France is left to boast the production of the most imposingly noble woman with whom history has made us acquainted.

We are aware that many of our readers will altogether dispute the principles by which we are induced to attribute such an eminence to a woman who was nothing more than a woman, holding the old orthodox rank of the "weaker vessel," and *as such* claiming peculiar honour; who was too much attached to her friends ever to soar quite out of the region of personalities; whose virtues were never startling, being all strung like pearls upon the silken thread of *propriety;* who was not without that amiable vanity which enhances our admiration by seeming not ungrateful for it; who, in fine, though virtuous and heroic when occasion required, was at all times and on all occasions nothing so much as womanly. Many others have been as virtuous, as beautiful, and as heroic; but none else has in an equal degree glorified these perfections by such an attractive radiance of *womanhood*,—that mysterious influence, which we can only describe by negatives and contradictions; that charming subordination, which affects us less as the necessity of a weaker being than as the complaisance of a nature which would rather persuade than command; that flattering inferiority, which allows us the leadership in wisdom, and is content that we should preach, so that it maintains the monopoly of the good example; that ever-present and ever-intangible charm, whose best praise is that it is the reverse of manhood. Marie de Hautefort has taught us what a woman may be, and what a man may aspire to deserve.

We gladly take the opportunity of repeating, in connection with her life, what M. Guizot says, in concluding his beautiful essay on Lady Russell, called "L'Amour dans le Mariage":

"I have felt profound pleasure in relating the history of this lady, so pure in her passion, always great, and always humble in her greatness, faithful and devoted, with equal ardour to her feelings and her duties in grief and joy, in triumph and adversity. Our times are attacked with a deplorable malady; men believe only in the passion which is attended with moral derangement: infinite love, perfect devotion, all ardent, exalted, and soul-mastering sentiments, appear to them impossible within the bounds of moral laws and social conventions; all order seems to them a paralysing yoke, all submission a debasing servitude; no flame is anything if it is not a devouring conflagration. This disease is all the graver because it is not the crisis of a fever, nor the explosion of an exuberant force. It springs from perverse doctrines, from the rejection of law, faith, and superhuman existence, from the idolatry of man, who takes himself for God. And with this disease there is joined another no less lamentable: man not only adores nothing but himself; but even himself he adores only in the multitude where all men are confounded. He hates and envies everything that rises above the vulgar level; all superiority, all individual grandeur, seems to him an iniquity and an injury towards that chaos of undistinguished and ephemeral beings whom he calls humanity. When he perceives, in the higher walks of society, some great scandal, some odious instance of vice and crime, he rejoices, and ardently turns it to the worst account against social superiorities, making it to be believed that such things are the natural consequences of high birth, great fortune, aristocratic condition. When we have been assailed by these base doctrines, and the shameful passions which give birth to, or are born from, them; when we have felt the hatefulness of them and measured the peril, it is a very lively delight to meet with one of those noble examples which are their splendid confutation. In proportion as I respect humanity in its totality, I admire and love those glorified images of humanity, which personify and set on high, under visible features and with a proper name, whatever it has of most noble and most pure. Lady Russell gives the soul this beautiful and virtuous joy. *C'est une grande dame chrétienne.*" And if Lady Russell and Madame de Hautefort are splendid and unanswerable replies to vulgar depreciations of aristocracy, they offer no less forcible and illustrious denials of the calumnies on womanhood which with our generation pass for praise. Of all the monstrous births of modern philosophy, surely none is so monstrous, so marked with *moral* ignorance and deterioration, as the doctrine of the equality of man and woman, in the form in which it is at present widely preached. No woman, who has read the foregoing pages, will suspect us of desiring to derogate from her honour; and, indeed, our indignation is, not so much because the doctrine in point diminishes the honour of man, as because it sullies by misrepresenting that of his gentle ally. Surely she has points of superiority enough, without disputing the sole points which we and nature deny to her— namely, wisdom for the legislative, and force for the executive, in life. Well aware that we really abuse what we overrate, we yet deliberately admit an excellency of nature in woman which puts to the blush the best results of grace in man. Her superiority to man in that wherein he most excels the beasts, religion; his physical inferiority to her in almost everything but that in which the beasts excel him, strength; the only virtue in which she does not share being that in which they do, physical courage; her far greater readiness to rejoice with them that do rejoice, and weep with them that weep; her infinite versatility, which caused an old writer to say: "Sing of the nature of woman, and then the song shall be surely full of varieties, old crotchets, and most sweet closes,—it shall be humour grave, fantastic, loving, melancholy, sprightly, one in all and all in one"; her beauty, which is love visible, which purifies our passions in exciting them, and makes our desires glow like sunny clouds in the sky of a pure conscience; her voice, which is audible benevolence; her manner, a miracle of lovely tact, and candour subtly-paced as guile;—these and other praises, which would exhaust us long before we exhausted them, are surely enough to countervalue that poor predominance of power with which the brain and muscles of man are indefeasibly endowed, and which force kingship upon him in the very teeth of his false philosophy. The happiness and dignity of man and woman require, not a confusion, but a complete distinction, of their relations; and the title of the "weaker vessel," being, on the best authority, the woman's peculiar title to honour, is not to be forgotten and ignored, but contemplated and loved. Only thus can their absolutely infinite capability of being mutually exalted come into effect. They are like the two plates of the philosophical instrument called the electrical doubler, which by mutual opposition under proper circumstances indefinitely intensify their contrasted conditions: her softness, delicacy, tenderness, compliance, fear, and confidence, opposed to whatever strength, courage, gravity, firmness, dignity, and originality there may have been in him before, render a certain exaltation of these virtues, for her sake, easy; every such exaltation upon his part induces in her a more passionate submission, whereby her peculiar qualities are correspondingly developed; and every such increment of loving and intelligent self-devotion calls upon him, in turn, for the delightful exercise of a higher degree of manhood, in order that he may deserve it. How hopeful would be that reform which should begin where life begins, in the relation of the sexes! How hopeless all reforms which attempt to clear the social current anywhere but at its source! There are certain moral processes which seem to be antecedent to religion. St. Paul tells us that the man who does not provide for those of his own household has not only denied the faith, but "*is worse than an infidel*"; and religion does not so much teach as assume a knowledge of the primary *facts* of nature, which those, who in our day are worse than infidels, represent as *doctrines*, in order that it may be possible to deny them. The family titles are those by which God reveals His relation to us and ours to Him; and to misinterpret them is to obscure revelation in its very terms. The human affections are the living figures by which we are to be taught to comprehend and feel those which are divine. The performance of natural duties, and the possession of natural knowledge, constitute and indicate that "honest and good heart," which we are told is not the fruit of the seed of faith, but the ground in which it must be sown, in order to come to perfection. Now the relation of man and woman, besides being the first and strongest of human ties, is the source from which they all spring; and a miscomprehension of the nature of the primary relation necessarily involves error in the understanding of those which are derivative.

XXII

MRS. MEYNELL

AT rare intervals the world is startled by the phenomenon of a woman whose qualities of mind and heart seem to demand a revision of its conception of womanhood and an enlargement of those limitations which it delights in regarding as essentials of her very nature, and as necessary to her beauty and attractiveness as woman. She belongs to a species quite distinct from that of the typical sweet companion of man's life, the woman who is so sweet and so companiable, even because, as Thomas Aquinas affirms, " she is scarcely a reasonable creature." A Lady Jane Grey, a Mrs. Hutchinson, a Lady Rachel Russell, or a Madame de Hautefort is, however, not less but more womanly for owing her exceptional character to the possession of qualities which are usually the prerogative of the ideal man ; a fact which corroborates a theory, not unknown to philosophy and theology, that sex in the soul lies in aspect rather than in substance. "Spirits, at will," says Milton, "can either sex assume, or both"; and women of the grander type, who prefer their womanhood to the assertion of their right to a masculine attitude towards the world, have always had the world in worship at the feet of their greater and sweeter femininity.

"Originally," says Plato, "there were three sexes." The Church teaches the same thing. God is the great prototype and source of sex: the Father being the original masculine intellect, the Word its feminine reflection, consciousness, or 'glory," while the Holy Spirit is defined to be "the embrace," or synthesis, "of the Father and the Word," the *Creator Spiritus*, that aspect (*Persona*) of God (who is "one in substance") which is the immediate source of all life, love, joy, and power. In man, the express image of God, *genius* is that divine third, quickening, and creative sex, which contains and is the two others, and which is so rare, owing to the loss of balance in man's nature, that Plato speaks of it as no longer existing.

In the realms of art and letters genius is, in its initial stage, perceptive reason, the rare power of seeing self-evident things; and its modes of expression correspond with its character. A strong and predominatingly masculine mind has often much to say, but a very imperfect ability to say it : the predominatingly feminine mind can say anything, but has nothing to say ; but with the double-sexed insight of genius, realities and expressions are wedded from their first conception, and, even in their least imposing developments, are living powers, and of more practical importance than the results of the highest efforts of mind when either of its factors greatly predominates over the other.

I am about to direct the reader's attention to one of the very rarest products of nature and grace—a woman of genius, one who, I am bound to confess, has falsified the assertion which I made some time ago, that no female writer of our time had attained to true " distinction." In the year 1875, Miss Alice Thompson (now Mrs. Meynell), the sister of Miss Thompson (Lady Butler), the painter of the famous " Roll Call," published a volume of poems, which were as near to being poetry as any woman of our time, with the exception perhaps of Miss Christina Rossetti, has succeeded in writing. But though this volume, in the opinion of some critics—Ruskin, D. G. Rossetti, Aubrey de Vere, and myself among others— far surpassed the work of far more famous " poetesses," it was not poetry in the sense which causes all real poets, however subordinate in their kind, to rank as immortals. There is sufficient intellect and imagination in Mrs. Meynell's Poems to have supplied a hundred of that splendid insect, Herrick; enough passion and pure human affection for a dozen poets like Crashaw or William Barnes; they breathe, in every line, the purest *spirit* of womanhood, yet they have not sufficient force of that *ultimate* womanhood, the expressional *body*, to give her the right to be counted among classical poets. No woman ever has been such a poet: probably no woman ever will be, for (strange paradox!) though, like my present subject, she may have enough and to spare of the virile intellect, and be also exquisitely womanly, she has not womanhood enough.

The feminine factor in the mind of the great poet is, indeed, a greater thing than woman—it is goddess. Keats and Shelley, in their best works, were wholly feminine; they were merely exponents of sensitive beauty; but into this they had such an insight, and with it such a power of self-identification, as no woman has ever approached. Mrs. Meynell's verses are full of delicate and original thought, for the most part faultlessly expressed. Witness this sonnet, called "Renouncement," which has deservedly found a place in most of our many modern anthologies:—

"I must not think of thee; and tired yet strong
I shun the thought that lurks in all delight—
The thought of thee—and in the blue heaven's height.
And in the sweetest passage of a song.
Oh, just beyond the fairest thoughts that throng
This breast, the thought of thee waits, hidden yet bright;
But it must never, never come in sight;
I must stop short of thee the whole day long.
But when sleep comes to close each difficult day,
When night gives pause to the long watch I keep,
And all my bonds I needs must loose apart,
Must doff my will as raiment laid away,—
With the first dream that comes with the first sleep
I run, I run, I am gather'd to thy heart."

This, like all Mrs. Meynell's verse, is true, beautiful, tender, and, negatively, almost faultless; but it does not attain the classical standard. Compared with that which is classical in the writings of second or even third-rate poets, like Herrick, Crashaw, and William Barnes, it is "as moonlight unto sunlight." Our admiration is, indeed, strongly awakened by it, but we think of and admire the poetess still more than her poetry. It does not strain to rival man's work, as Mrs. Browning's does, nor to put forth the great, impersonal claims of great poetry, nor claim to have mastered the arduous *technique* whereby every phrase becomes a manifold mystery of significance and music. Mrs. Meynell's thoughts and feelings seem to be half-suffocated by their own sweetness and pathos, so that, though they can speak with admirable delicacy, tenderness, and—that rarest of graces—unsuperfluousness, they cannot sing. With extraordinary power of self-judgment, she discovered this fact while she was as yet a mere girl, and, disdaining to do anything which she could not do, not only well, but best, and notwithstanding the encouragement to persevere in poetry which she received from a large and high class of critics, she gave up the attempt, and has hardly since written a line.

But, in a very small volume of very short essays, which she has just published, this lady has shown an amount of perceptive reason and ability to discern self-evident things as yet undiscerned, a reticence, fulness, and effectiveness of expression, which place her in the very front rank of living writers in prose. The greater part of this little volume is *classical* work, embodying, as it does, new thought of general and permanent significance in perfect language, and bearing, in every sentence, the hall-mark of genius, namely, the marriage of masculine force of insight with feminine grace and tact of expression. Of the "sweetness and wit," which are said, by Donne, I think, to be woman's highest attainment, there is in these little essays abundance, but they are only the living drapery of thought which has the virile qualities of simplicity, continuity, and positiveness. The essays of Emerson, of which those of Mrs. Meynell will sometimes remind the reader, are not to be compared with the best of hers in these greater merits; moreover, the "transcendentalism" of the American writer afforded a far easier field than that chosen by the English lady. It is very easy to speak splendidly and profusely about things which transcend speech; but to write beautifully, profitably, and originally about truths which come home to everybody, and which everybody can test by common sense; to avoid with sedulous reverence the things which are beyond the focus of the human eye, and to direct attention effectively to those which are well within it, though they have hitherto been undiscerned through lack of attention, or the astounding imperfection of common vision for the reality of common things, is a very different attainment. Gaiety of manner with gravity of matter, truth perceived clearly and expressed with ease and joy, constitute the very highest and rarest of prose writing. Emerson had no gravity and no true sequence of thought, for he lived or attempted to live in a sphere in which the laws of gravitation do not operate, and which, being without limitation, is without unity. In the writing of Mrs. Meynell we have brightness and epigram enough, but they are but the photosphere of weighty, intelligible, and simple human interest; and they never tempt her, as the possession of such wit almost inevitably tempts the male writer, to any display of scorn and contempt. She has always pity and palliatory explanation for the folly or falsehood which she exposes so trenchantly. Perhaps the unkindest hit in her book is that in which she laughs at the New-Worldling, thus :—

"The difficulty of dealing, in the course of any critical duty, with decivilised man lies in this: when you accuse him of vulgarity—sparing him, no doubt, the word—he defends himself against the charge of barbarism. Especially from new soil—transatlantic, colonial—he faces you, bronzed, with a half conviction of savagery, partly persuaded of his own youthfulness of race. He writes and recites poems about ranches and canyons; they are designed to betray the recklessness of his nature, and to reveal the good that lurks in the lawless ways of a young society. He is there to explain himself, voluble with a glossary for his own artless slang. But his colonialism is only provincialism very articulate. The new air does but make old decadences seem more stale; the young soil does but set into fresh conditions the ready-made, the uncostly, the refuse feeling of a race decivilising. American fancy played long this pattering part of youth. The New Englander hastened to assure you with so self-denying a face he did not wear war-paint and feathers, that it became doubly difficult to communicate to him that you had suspected him of nothing wilder than a second-hand dress-coat."

In this last phrase, as in all Mrs. Meynell's wit, the razor-edge cuts so keenly because of the weight at its back. In one little sentence she shatters a world of pretension which, without deceiving anyone, has puzzled most of us in the attempt to define and dissipate it; and henceforward we shall never be without an answer to the worn-out and vulgarised civilisee when he at once boasts of and apologises for being a fine young savage.

The title of the essay which contains the passage I have quoted is a word invented by Mrs. Meynell, and not before it was wanted. We had "uncivilised" and "over-civilised," but no word to express the condition in which "Progress" has at last landed the world, especially the English-speaking part of it. The epithet "decivilised" is in itself an achievement of insight, and a word to conjure by.

"Decivilised man," continues our authoress, "is not peculiar to new soil. The English town, too, knows him in all his dailiness. In England, too, he has a literature, an art, a music, all his own, derived from many and various things of price. Trash, in the fulness of its insimplicity and cheapness, is impossible without a beautiful past. Its chief characteristic—which is futility, not failure—could not be achieved but by the long abuse, the rotatory reproduction, the quotidian disgrace, of the utterances of art, especially the utterance by words. Gaiety, vigour, vitality, the organic quality, purity, simplicity, precision—all these are among the antecedents of trash. . . . The decivilised have every grace as the antecedent of their vulgarities, every distinction as the precedent of their mediocrities. No ballad-concert song, feign it sigh, frolic, or laugh, but has the excuse that the feint was suggested, was made easy, by some once living sweetness. Nor are the decivilised to blame as having in their own persons possessed civilisation and marred it. They did not possess it ; they were born into some tendency to derogation, into an inclination for things mentally inexpensive. And the tendency can hardly do other than continue. Nothing can look duller than the future of this secondhand and multiplying world."

Where, in the whole field of modern literature, can we find a more significant, original, and convincing piece of writing than this ?

In the way of art-criticism very few have equalled Mrs. Meynell's little essay on Velasquez, whom she calls "the first Impressionist." In this essay she, for the first time, and with the extreme brevity and fulness of genius, explains and justifies Impressionism, and abolishes the pretensions of almost all modern " Impressionists " to their self-assumed title. The best of this lady's essays, which seldom run to greater length than about five or six pages, are so perfect that to give extracts as samples is like chipping off corners of "specimen" rubies or emeralds for the like purpose. Their value is not in arithmetical, but in geometrical, proportion to their bulk. Since, however, there is no room for the whole ruby, take this chip from the "Point of Honour."

"Not without significance is the Spanish nationality of Velasquez. In Spain was the point put upon honour; and Velasquez was the first Impressionist. As an Impressionist he claimed, implicitly if not explicitly, a whole series of delicate trusts in his trustworthiness. . . . He kept the chastity of art when other masters were content with its honesty, and when others saved artistic conscience he safeguarded the point of honour. Contemporary masters more or less proved their position, and convinced the world by something of demonstration; the first Impressionist simply asked that his word should be accepted. To those who will not take his word he offers no bond. To those who will he grants the distinction of a share in his responsibility. Somewhat unrefined, in comparison with his lofty and simple claim to be believed on a suggestion, is the commoner painter's production of his credentials, his appeal to the sanction of ordinary experience, his self-defence against the suspicion of making irresponsible mysteries in art. 'You can see for yourself,' the lesser man seems to say to the world; 'thus things are, and I render them in such manner that your intelligence may be satisfied.' This is an appeal to average experience, at the best to cumulative experience, and with the average or the sum, art cannot deal without derogation. The Spaniard seems to say, 'Thus things are in my pictorial sight. Trust me: I apprehend them so.' We are not excluded from his councils, but we are asked to attribute a certain authority to him, master of the craft as he is, master of that art of seeing pictorially which is the beginning and not far from the end—not far short of the whole—of the art of painting. So little, indeed, are we shut out from the mysteries of a great Impressionist's impression, that Velasquez requires us to be in some degree his colleagues. Thus may each of us to whom he appeals take praise from the praised. He leaves my educated eyes to do a little of the work. He respects my responsibility no less—though he respects it less explicitly —than I do his. . . . Because Impressionism is so free, therefore is it so doubly bound. To undertake this art for the sake of its privileges, without confessing its obligations, or at least without confessing them up to the point of honour, is to take a vulgar freedom; to see immunities precisely where there are duties. A very mob of men have taken Impressionism upon themselves in this our later day. It is against all probabilities that more than a few among these have within them the point of honour. . . . May the gods guard us from the further popularising of Impressionism; for the point of honour is the simple secret of the few."

In no other authoress of this century can anything be positively inferred, concerning the character of the writer, from her works; but there breathes from almost every paragraph and stanza of these two little volumes the indefinable but unmistakable perfume of a sweet, noble, and singular personality. Mrs. Meynell's style is like the subtle and convincing commentary of a beautiful voice.

The range of subject in this score of miniature essays is very large, and an extraordinary degree of finished culture in various directions is displayed, with an entire absence of pretension or even consciousness. "The Rhythm of Life," "A Remembrance," "The Sun," "The Flower," "By the Railway Side," "Composure," "Domus Angusta," "Rejection," "Innocence and Experience," "Decivilised," "The Point of Honour," bear no resemblance one to the other, except in their equal charm of fulness, brevity, original insight, experience, graceful learning, and unique beauty of style. The authoress never falls below the high standard she has attained in the two essays I have now quoted, except in cases in which she has chosen matter unworthy of her powers. The merits of Lowell and Oliver Wendell Holmes, and the vulgarity of Dickens and the caricaturists of fifty years ago, may afford very good subjects for ordinary critics, but diamond-dust and a razor-edge, though it may have the weight of a hatchet behind it, are quite unadapted for the working up of blocks of teak or sandstone. There is a sort of sanctity about such delicate genius as Mrs. Meynell's which makes one shrink to see the robe of her Muse brush against anything common.

Let her respect her own graceful powers and personality, as every man of true delicacy and insight must respect them, and she will become one of the fairest and steadiest lights of English literature, though she may remain unconspicuous to "the crowd, incapable of perfectness."

XXIII

DIEU ET MA DAME

WOMAN is the last and lowest of all spiritual creatures; made "a little lower than the angels" to be "crowned with the glory and honour" of being the final and visible reflection of the beauty of God, which in itself no eye shall ever otherwise see; for "the beatific vision," as St. Bernard says, "is not a thing that is seen, but a substance which is sucked, as through a nipple." The Blessed Virgin, "the holiest and humblest of creatures," crowned with the glory and honour of bearing God in her womb, is the one woman in whom womanhood has been perfected, and in whom the whole of womanhood has been more or less reconstituted and glorified.

But though woman has thus been glorified by an inconceivably higher circumstance of honour than man, and has been made and declared to be not only "Regina Mundi" but "Regina Cœli," man, in the order of being, is and will for ever be above her. He, as man, seems to be, in some sort, the last of the angelic order, being not only a reflection but also a transmitter and messenger of the Divine original Fatherhood, represented to the Blessed Virgin herself in St. Joseph. Theology teaches that a characteristic of all the angelic orders is the capacity of assuming a double aspect. They can turn their gaze directly upon God, a state which St. Thomas Aquinas describes as the "Morning Joy," or they can turn to God in his creature, which is said to be the "Evening Joy." The Father alone looks for ever downward, and the woman alone for ever upward, "her angel always beholding the face" of the original divinity; and, in whatever order an angelic substance may stand, all orders below and above are, as it were, transparent, the vision of each ending, in one direction, in the Father, and, in the other, in the Woman, that opaque surface in which the rays of Deity end, and from which they are reflected in all the multiplied splendours which they have gathered by being transmitted through the prismatic and refractive spheres that intervene. In this duplicate order, each angelic entity represents and contains the Divine Fatherhood for the entity next below, and the womanhood, its "glory" for that next above; a fact which Milton seems to have discerned, without the aid of Catholic theology, when he wrote

> "Spirits at will
> Can either sex assume;"

and which every "Bride of Christ" who is also a pure and ardent Lover discerns, when his eyes are first opened, as by a deific flash, to the feminine splendour, and he feels that "Dieu et ma Dame" is no irreverent or hyperbolic legend for his double but not divided worship. The ideal womanhood, which only one woman has realised fully, but which every woman seems to be capable of more or less representing to some man, for at least one moment in his life, is the photosphere of God, the light and joy of the universe, "Regina Mundi," as the glory of nature, and "Regina Cœli" when she shall have become nature glorified.

Man, then, as soon as he is made by grace a participator of angelic and celestial powers, stands between God and woman, and, as he pleases and when he pleases, can take aspect as Bride to Christ or bridegroom to woman, the Priestess of the Divine Truth or Beauty to him, as he is Priest of the Divine Love or Power to her.

To render this, the central fact of life, conceivable and credible to such as have not attained to knowledge, those who know have remarked certain analogies, say rather identities of Divine and human love, of which, from reading and hearing whereof I have kept no exact notes, I will give a few examples.

The doctrine of election, which is such that it can neither be accepted nor denied by the understanding, has its lively image in "the way of a man with a maid," which, also, Solomon himself confessed that he could not understand. The man sees many maids, often of much more apparent beauty and merit than the one he chooses; and, in his choice of her, there is no compulsion. He may feel attracted by somewhat in her, but he is not in love with her, until by an act of will, he abandons his will, and assumes, by a distinct act of election, a state of mind towards her from which thenceforward he is unable to withdraw himself, whereby it becomes her manifest fault if she does not "make her election sure" by offering no such violence to love as must inevitably cause divorce.

Again, the Divine Lover, like a wise mortal lover, knows well that, however favourably the Soul may be disposed to Him, by His greatness, power, wealth, goodness, and abundant benevolence to her, He must *desire* her, and give her some sensible proof by smile, touch, or caress, which shall say to her heart, as the God of David says to the chosen, "Rex concupiscet decorem tuum."

Again, God's strength, like man's, is perfected in weakness. When the Soul has entered upon her third and crowning stage of perfection and union, His divine weakness for her gives Him far more influence over her will than would be obtained by any display of His power and other attributes. As with a mortal lover, there is, as some one has said, an appearance of infatuation in the love of God for the elect soul. Though just and beneficent to others, He has nothing but boundless indulgence for her. "If she loves," says Saint Augustine, "she may do as she likes." He will forgive her, almost without asking, all faults short of wilful and persistent infidelity, and, since she herself hates them, He even loves her the more for them. What ardent lover but knows that the present faults and shortcomings of the beloved are condiments and excitations of the appetite of love, impediments in the current of his passion which only render its self-willed and self-rejoicing force more sensible and triumphant? And past corruptions that are really past and no longer active are so far from hindering love that they act as manure in which the seed of Divine Love and the seed almost divine of a pure and fervid mortal affection flourish wonderfully, many a Magdalen, the just envy of many who were always pure, having been formed into a spouse, "more innocent than any maid," by the inveterate and purifying ardour of either love.

Again, as with a mortal lover, God does not require any service of external "charity," etc., from His beloved. Indeed, He complains, as He did to Martha, of all attempts to please Him otherwise than by giving Him her society and her person, in contemplation. "All," says St. Francis of Sales, "must serve her" (the elect Soul), "but she must serve none, not even her Divine Lover, of whom she is not a servant but spouse." He reproves in her the kind of humility which He requires of others, in whom He has not yet inspired that perfection of intention which in her He regards as attainment. He also requires in her, as a mortal lover does, that amount of "vanity," as the world calls it, which sees and rejoices in her own beauty; for it is only her knowledge of her own loveliness in His eyes which makes His love credible to her, and it is only her belief in His love which enables her to give that perfect response of feeling which is love's fruition, and causes her beauty to brighten more and more in the joy of His flatteries, making her "sweet to herself who is so sweet to Him."

Again, in either love, the one party retains a

power of absolute command, which he never uses, while the other has an equal force of persuasion, of which she avails herself abundantly. She delights in calling herself his slave; he delights in being hers, and in boasting himself a "servant of servants."

A mysterious longing for corporeal and spiritual captivity to the beloved animates either kind of love—if, indeed, they be not really one in kind. In love, the woman, who is "the body," desires to be utterly captive to the man's will, and he, in return, to be utterly captive to her body. His soul lives in and is moved blissfully by every turn of her head and motion of her limbs. He already is carried hither and thither in all her movements, although he is not yet *numerically* one flesh with her; but this is much more so with the Divine Lover, who actually enjoys that distinctness in identity to which the mortal lover only and for ever in vain aspires, namely, to be "man compassed by a woman," as Isaiah says, speaking of that Incarnation which is effected more or less in each of the elect, as in Jesus Himself perfectly. These two captivities constitute one freedom, and every look and gesture of the beloved is a sacrament and a common joy. As I have said elsewhere—

"'Tis but in such captivity
The heavens themselves know what they be."

Another remarkable point in this divine analogy is the reciprocal desire of the great for the small and the small for the great. An ordinary man requires in his mistress abilities corresponding to his own, and he who cannot love much commonly demands from her a great power of love for him. A great man has a wilful and somewhat amused delight ("Olla subridens") in binding himself in wedlock to one who, indeed, implicitly believes in his greatness, but who is really nothing but a little, ignorant Love, who gives all her mite and understands only caresses. To a great man and to a God a little love is a great thing. As the greatest of souls is infinitely little to God, it follows that this peculiar source of felicity in extremes is, in the divine marriage, unfathomable and inexhaustible.

Another phenomenon common to both kinds of love is the longing—almost the first that arises in every true lover's bosom—to die for the sake of the beloved. "I have longed for this hour," said Our Lord. But none, save God, can die and yet live for her.

Again, between lovers, things which, under ordinary relationships, are only "counsels of perfection," become obligatory duties; the least inattention is almost a mortal offence, raising a cloud of separation which nothing but bitter penance and greater devotion than ever can dissipate; so that the spouse of God may well suspect the reality of her position, if her life, in this world, is not fuller of sorrows than of smiles, and if her failures have not rendered her perfection sensibly greater this week than it was last.

Again, in human as in divine love, "a part is greater than the whole," and either love finds its fruition in sacraments or symbols, which are parts representing the whole. Even in the presence of the beloved, the lover will choose to fix his soul upon a ribbon or a lock of hair, intensifying his apprehension of a too numerous and overwhelming beauty by thus focusing it on one point. Another of the many paradoxes common to both loves is, that they can see best in the dark. "Night is the light of my pleasures."

Again, since, in this life, the wedlock of God and the soul is, at best, only in its first stage or betrothal, its felicities, to the soul at least, are, as with the betrothed maiden, defective, full of unintelligible and impatient desires, and daily mingled with the almost intolerable miseries of temporary separation, which seems eternal, for, while it lasts, she cannot see her own beauty, which only exists for her in the light of His countenance. When thus He withdraws from her, she becomes in her own eyes vile, unmeaning, and unlovely as the sheath of a lost sword, or the cast skin of a serpent, and it is impossible at such times to give a sensible belief to the certainty that she will, ere long, be again alive with His life and splendid with the reflection of His complacency.

Another most notable analogy of love is the revelation, completion, and explanation of herself which the lover in either case brings to the beloved. She is as the fragment of a "puzzle-picture," until she encounters the destined complement of her being, and the key to her unintelligible dreams. They then suddenly become such realities as make all other realities dreams. She dares not believe or accept the wonders of her position until she discerns that acceptance of them is imposed on her by duty and faith. Then she can no more doubt that, through all the range of her constitution, she is the blissful reciprocal of him whom she adores, than she could doubt of her own existence, which, indeed, without him, would now be no existence. In him is the only possible satisfaction of her rational, voluntary, and sensitive life, and she attains to fathomless content in the extremes of reverence for and intimacy with him.

But this is perhaps the greatest and most inscrutable of all the mysteries common to either kind of love—there is, in its felicity, the coexistence of a celestial and exceedingly virginal pride with an insatiable appetite for its surrender and sacrifice. Theologians say that the essential of the Sacrifice of the Altar is the infinite humiliation suffered by the Second Person of the Holy Trinity in becoming flesh in the moment of transubstantiation; and has not this humiliation its analogue in the case of the Virgin when she allows her love and beauty, thitherto nothing but spiritual splendour and ethereal freedom, to become the ally and thrall of the body?

The last of the innumerable analogies, or rather identities, which I shall here notice is the indissolubility of union, when it has reached its final stage. So long as love in the soul is only in the initial state of light, or assent to and admiration of what is most excellent, the light may be quenched by other lights, less pure and bright, but nearer; when, again, the light descends into the will, this may not be able to bear the strain of a love that calls for continual fidelity of correspondence; but when it reaches the sensible affections and has been crowned in mutual and ineffable complacencies, there is no longer any practical danger of separation. The Soul feels assured that, above and apart from the great security she enjoys in the fact that all temptation has been cut up at the roots by her possession of a sensible and abiding felicity which makes all others insipid, and which enables her to say, with full sincerity, "Whom have I in Heaven but Thee, and what on earth in comparison with Thee," her Lord also has entered into new relations with her, and she is relieved of obligations, while He has assumed them. He wants nothing of her now which she does not delight to give; whereas He has taken on Him the marital duty of seeing that all temptation which could endanger her is kept at a distance; He is bound to cherish and comfort, and behave, not with justice, but with tender indulgence to His own flesh; and, in case of any occasional weakness of obedience on her part, to show Himself the loving Master that she loves Him to be, by *compelling* her sensitive disinclination to such external duties as may remain. He has now made her "holy" or "separate" to Himself, and "He will not suffer His Holy One to see corruption." His mercies are now "the *sure* mercies of David," and though she acknowledges that there is still a hypothetical possibility of divorce should she fall, as it is practically incredible that she now can, a possibility that causes her to "rejoice with trembling," yet, on the whole, she is "*sure* that neither death, nor life, nor angels, nor principalities, nor powers, nor things present, nor things to come, nor height, nor depth, nor any other creature," shall be able to separate her from her Love.

This parallel appears to fail in one point; I mean, the extreme jealousy on the part of the Divine Lover of the Soul, when once she has entered upon this relationship to Him, and the entire absence of jealousy on her part. Sleep and accidental and external duty do not separate her from Him, but the least waking thought, feeling, word, or act, which has not Him, directly or indirectly, for its object, does. When God makes Himself as wine to the Beloved, like the fabled Bacchus the one thing He resents is inattention, and when she has fallen into this offence, she has to recover her favour with Him by tears and prayers. She, however, is not only content but delighted to think that there are many whom He loves as well or better than He loves her. I attribute this fact to her instinctive perception that her beauty is unique ("there is none like her, none"), and that no other can ever be to Him what she is, though millions may be a great deal more. Moreover, by virtue of the supernatural elevation of her intellect in her intimacies with Him, she is enabled to discern that He has the power of absolutely forgetting all others when she is in His presence, and that He is, at such times, wholly hers; a concrete fact which the philosophers express in the abstract, when they affirm that "God is a circle whose centre is everywhere and circumference nowhere."

Perhaps—but I am not sure, for I do not know the mind of women or that of the Saints well enough to judge—the parallel also fails in this, that, in the higher relationship, the soul is always more or less troubled by the incredibility of so much bliss and honour, and, in the presence of the only reality of life, a reality as natural as it is spiritual, she perpetually sighs—

> "Ah, me, I do not dream,
> Yet all this does some heathen fable seem!"

With these exceptions, if exceptions they be, there is, indeed, *no* vital characteristics of a perfectly ordered love, in the natural sphere, which has not its likeness and full development in the Divine; nor can even the natural perfection of love be attained, without habitual reference to the spiritual. Wordsworth says:

> "By grace divine,
> Not otherwise, O Nature, are we thine,"

and a man can only love a woman with full felicity by understanding and obeying Christ's injunction that he should love her as He loves the Church, which every lover of God is in little, "The woman for the man," "the man by the woman," and "God all in all" in both:—for Milton's rule,

"He for God only, she for God in him,"

is not a wholly adequate statement of the relationship of man and woman, though it is as near a statement as a Socinian could be expected to arrive at. The woman is "homo" as well as the man, though one element, the male, is suppressed and quiescent in her, as the other, the female, is in him; and thus he becomes the Priest and representative to her of the original Fatherhood, while she is made to him the Priestess and representative of that original Beauty which is "the express image and glory of the Father," each being equally, though not alike, a manifestation of the Divine to the other.

Love, with this commentary on it written in the hearts of lovers, becomes as much brighter, purer, and more ardent than the love which is without it as the electric light is brighter, purer, and more ardent than a torch of tar; and so far is it from being true, as the foolish might imagine, that something of the natural delight of love must be lost in this its exaltation, that everything which is truly in Nature's order gains immensely by the supernatural heat and light which illuminate and purge the exceeding obscurity of the phenomena of the uninformed natural passion.

Should any believing reader object that such thoughts as I have suggested to him imply an irreverent idea of the intimacies of God with His elect, I beg him to remember that in receiving the Blessed Sacrament with the faith which the Church demands, he affirms and *acts* a familiarity which is greater than any other that can be conceived.

For more of these analogies the reader may consult the verses called "De Natura Deorum," in the *Unknown Eros.*

If any one perseveres in the path of perfection, these points of likeness between Divine and human love will become *res cognita et visa;* and he will see that the phenomena of the human relationship of love are such because they are the realities of the Divine. For all properly human instincts are no other than the lineaments of God; and man (*homo*) is an image and likeness of God, most especially in those mysteries which—let all remark well—are quite as inscrutable in their secondary, or human, as in their primary manifestation, "the surest foundation of marriage-love being," as Hooker says, "that of which we are least able to render a reason."

Let none who have as yet had no experience of these things, though they may have been doing their very best, despair. We must usually feed for many years upon divine things before God gives us the taste of our food; and even when we have done all, we may not find ourselves among the blessed number of those who are called to the Counsels of Perfection, and the fruition of God in this life.

THE END

Printed by R. & R. CLARK, *Edinburgh*

www.ingramcontent.com/pod-product-compliance
Lightning Source LLC
Chambersburg PA
CBHW022008220426
43663CB00007B/1012